Managing Balances for Peace in Our Life, Country, and World

We can learn from recession, conflict, and war

John H. Lee

ISBN-10: 1475045123

ISBN-13: 978-1475045123

Library of Congress Control Number: 2012905110

DEDICATION

This book is dedicated to my wife, Jane,
and to my children Angela and Richard.

CONTENTS

John H. Lee

ACKNOWLEDGMENTS

To my wife, Jane, for her support, patience, and willingness to spend countless hours with me over the last twenty years.

To Erwin Clark, Jake Combs, and Angela Lee, for their assistance.

PREFACE

The United States and the world have been facing a serious recession after 2007. Many companies and people have had bankruptcies. There have been serious problems from the housing mortgage market to insurance companies and the financial management of Wall Street. Companies then had to cut employment, purchasing power was reduced significantly, and millions of people lost their jobs. The recession of 2008 and 2009 have affected many people in the United States and other countries. It is one of the most serious recessions in our history, causing many layoffs and house foreclosures. In 2009, the overall poverty rate was 14.3 percent, which was equivalent to 43.6 million people, meaning one of every seven Americans was in poverty. The 2009/2010 poverty level was about $22,000/year for a family of four, based on a calculation that includes only cash income, before tax deductions [1].

During this recession, there were many unbalances and conflicts in individuals, families, companies, societies, and countries, such as between income and expense, banks and home owners with foreclosures, employers and employees, government budget and national deficit, hunger and high priced food, and psychological depression and peace. This recession

1

officially ended in June 2009. However the recovery process is very slow. People still feel the strong effects of the recession in 2010, 2011, and 2012. Now our challenges are how to recover and reduce or even avoid recessions in the future

People have different positions, situations, attitudes, reviews, and philosophies. These differences often cause personal, social and international issues and problems without peace because of their own ideas, positions, benefits, and actions. People, communities, countries, and nations may have many conflicts. We need to overcome conflicts and have peace together. Looks major factors, which cause these recessions, conflicts and wars, are various unbalances in persons, families, countries, and the world.

When our balances are broken, problems, recessions, conflicts, and wars appear and even grow. The balance between income and expense is a basic and simple example. People, who spend more than their incomes, break the income-expense balance and cause various personal problems. The solution is to change their life style and have a balance between incomes, taxes, expenses, and savings. Overspending causes different problems for the individual as well as other people, who can be directly or indirectly related. Irresponsible actions may cause many problems. This book will discuss how to make balances for peace in the different areas of income, expense, personal life, time distribution, education, political parties, government policies, tax simplification, poor and rich people, immigration issues, religious and non-religious faiths, country development, and the world. We can make our balances for peace in our life, community, country, and world. Peace comes from balance. There is no peace without balance. There are simple and complex balances.

To achieve peace, people have to have balances. Peace for individuals, families, countries, and the world allow for more stable development at the lowest personal and social costs.

When people manage to balance more areas of their life, they will have more peace. When governments and government leaders manage their related balances for their countries and people, then related countries will have more peace and stability.

I hope this book allows people to think about how to balance many factors related to life, emotion, relationship, work, study, health, education, employment, budget, national interest, faith, conflict, country development, and many issues for individuals, families, communities, countries, and the world. I wish that people, government leaders, and countries would manage balances, leading to more peace in our life, countries, and world.

John Lee
johnlee1961@yahoo.com
June 4, 2012

John H. Lee

1. RECESSION SOLUTION AND BALANCE

Recession in 2008 and lesson

Only when a recession begins, many people, including government officers, recognize that they should spend less and save more. However less spending means less purchasing, which reduces production and causes even more layoffs during a recession. The government then has to help even more unemployed people by increasing the deficit and taxes. The ultimate result of less spending during a recession makes the recession even worse.

The crashing of home mortgages was the first sign of the recession of 2008, which was caused by some mortgage insurance companies, banks, agents, CEOs, homeowners, and governments, who all pushed for high-risk home loans. Most of the homeowners who cannot pay their mortgages on time or have had house foreclosures are unemployed or have been given impractical evaluations of their ability to pay their loans before they purchased their houses. The building materials from the house industry were over supplies and mortgage companies and banks provided the high-risk loans. Some agents and executives pushed for high-risk loans and mortgage insurance, transferring these high-risk loans to large mortgage companies for their own purposes to make more money, some of which were related cases to economic crimes, false information and over appraisal.

The changes in the housing industry caused the unbalance of many related industries, reducing production, and services, which caused even more unemployment. The unemployment proceeded to impede upon the ability of homeowners to pay their mortgages, especially those homeowners who had little to no down payment and not enough savings. The homeowners who were unemployed and the banks and mortgage companies who had these bad loans were serious victims. Mortgage insurance companies failed as more and more homeowners filed claims. It was not surprised that housing finance giants like Federal National Mortgage Association (Fannie Mae) and Federal Home Loan Mortgage Corporation (Freddie Mac), who both provided many high-risk loans and failed. Both of Fannie Mae and Freddie Mac were supported by the U.S. government. The problem was rooted in the executive teams, lobby interests, and former government officers. Before the recession, "short-term profits" were already distributed to related people in these banks, mortgage and mortgage insurance companies, lobbies, and former government officers. These executives got more incomes and bonuses. Once the recession came, they pushed the consequence to the government and the public. Our government and tax payers have begun to pay for the debts of these non-responsible companies, banks and executives. We need to take action to prevent non-responsible damages.

To avoid similar situations in the future, all parties need to be responsible for their own behaviors and duties, working together to prevent recessions in our future. Unrelated people became responsible for the serious economic situations and the financial crimes committed, which was one of the original reason people protested on Wall Street in October 2011. They went to protest about the unfairness of these financiers and corporation executives who caused the economic crisis, but then went on to accept government bailout and became even richer while other people have been left struggling with the recession and unemployment. It has become a rather large movement, spreading across the world. Of course protesters should respect traffic order, local regulations, laws, and other people who live and do business in that areas. Protesters need to have clear and specific missions and goals, allowing the related problems to have a chance of resolved. Otherwise related problems cannot be resolved. Protesters would even be seen as "trouble makers". Many movements lack clear and specific missions and goals, often losing control, causing damages and violence in the society.

Before this recession, many people and economists were concerned that mortgage companies were lending high-risk loans with very low or almost no down payment, such as 3%. In addition over appraisal and the acceptance of these high-risk loans by mortgage insurance companies were also of concern. Companies then transferred these high-risk loans and mortgage insurances to large companies such as Fannie Mae, Freddie Mac, and AIG. The CEOs and related workers in these companies received high incomes and bonuses. Wall Street was another area of investment abuse to investors. Many people were concerned that something bad would happen. But they could not do anything to these CEOs and fund managers. If the government suggested a minimum mortgage down payments, such as 10% or 15% for the government-supported Fannie Mae and Freddie Mac in 2005 or 2007, defining upper limits for management and service fees, and investigating cases to find economic crimes, then the housing mortgage crash, which caused the economic crisis of 2008, could have been reduced significantly or avoided. Investigations are needed for economic crimes and potential crimes. It was reported that the Securities and Exchange Commission charged six former top executives of the Fannie Mae and Freddie Mac in December of 2011 with securities fraud, alleging that they knew and approved of misleading statements that claimed the companies had minimal holdings of higher-risk mortgage loans, including subprime loans [2]. If the government had done similar investigations before 2007, then this recession could have been significantly reduced or even avoided.

It was reported that Fannie Mae's CEO and Freddie Mac's CEO, each received about $5.5 million in 2010. All the executives received a significant portion of their pay in the year or years after they earned it. The CEOs' pay targets were about $6 million for 2011. Freddie's CEO might not get much of that money because he announced to leave Freddie in 2012. He must still be in the company in order to receive the deferred compensation. His base pay for 2011 was $900,000, with most of the rest of his compensation coming in through deferred payments. Fannie Mae and Freddie Mac did bad performance to have many high-risk home loans and received government support. Why their CEOs still received very high incomes?

When companies accept government bailout funds or loans, their executive incomes and bonuses should be reduced significantly, such that they do not receive more than a certain amount, do not lay more people off (such as maximum 12%), use different methods, like reducing employee work time from five to four days/week, cutting salary 10% or selling part of the business to others until these companies back to normal operations, and return the funds or loans back to the government. It is not surprising for people to be mad at these CEOs who have salaries higher than 20, 50 or even 100 times the salaries of their average employees. These CEOs' are abusing their power as CEO to have very high salaries relatively. When CEOs' salaries are compared and set within a certain multiple of their average employee salary, CEOs may think about their employees as well.

It is beneficial to have inspection and protection systems to prevent or avoid serious economic crimes, like the case of

Bernard Madoff (the former Wall Street financier), who cost his victims more than $13 billion. He pled guilty to defrauding his clients and was sentenced 150 years in prison in June of 2009 [3]. What we can learn from these crimes? Before significant damages or potential significant damages occur, the government needs to protect national interests and the people, investigating related issues to avoid damages to the society and punish related executives, management teams, and individuals, who make crimes. Prevention costs the lowest social resources. Investors need to be more sensitive, having common senses to see things that are too good to be "true" and understand that there may be potential crimes behind "good" news. It is necessary to report current or potential economic crimes to the government. The Internal Revenue Service should audit more related significant investments, interests, capital gains, incomes, and profits from banks and companies. Large personal and company accounts, such as annual incomes above $500,000 for individuals or families and annual sales above $5 million for companies and organizations, should be suggested or required to have audit services from publically certified accounting firms. If there are significant differences or unbalances, more investigation is needed to prevent economic crimes, which would affect our society significantly.

Bernard Madoff apologized to his victims: "I have left a legacy of shame, as some of my victims have pointed out, to my family and my grandchildren. This is something I will live in for the rest of my life. I'm sorry." One of Bernard Madoff's victims committed suicide in December of 2008. Bernard Madoff's son, Mark Madoff, (46 years old) ended his life by suicide because of his father's situations and his body was found dead in his apartment on December 11, 2010 [4]. He left his wife and two-year-old son. All economic crimes will be discovered sooner or later. Those who are entertaining ideas of committing economic crimes or any crimes should consider the related punishments if discovered.

Principle and healthy balance

In a healthy situation, there is balance between income and spending, saving and potential spending capacity, production and sale/purchase, unemployment security funds and unemployment, and job creation/opportunity and investment. It is important to balance investment, employment, purchase, production, sale, profit, and reproduction. People and companies should spend certain levels in a recession to maintain basic production, employment, and purchase, which helps to recover from a recession.

During a recession, some people like our leaders or government to have a "magic" solution to overcome the related problems, resulting in more employment, purchases, and sales. They are absolutely not possible. People and their leaders need to work together from top to bottom and from bottom to top. The basic principles remain the same. Thousands of years ago, Joseph helped Pharaoh and people of Egypt in Bible. During the seven years of abundance the land produced plentifully, he asked people to collect the food produced in those seven years of abundance in Egypt. Huge quantities of grain were stored. Then the seven years of famine began. When the famine had spread over the whole country, Joseph and his people opened storehouses and sold grain to Egyptians. There also was famine in the other countries. People in the other countries went to Egypt to buy food items.

The principle is unchanged whether in the past, present, or future. People need to have emergency funds, savings, and assets, which can be used to overcome difficulties and recover from a recession. During good times, people, companies, and governments often mistakenly spend more with very little to no saving. During a recession, many people, companies, and the government, often become more conservative, spending less and saving more, which does not help the recovery process. This situation must be changed to avoid paying a higher price in the future. People, companies, and the government need to have certain funds set aside to sustain basic life needs, production, and services for a period of time in a recession.

The solution is for people to take responsibilities before, during, and after a recession, working together to create more jobs and opportunities at different levels through friendly government policies, using savings, making or borrowing money to cover daily expenses, keeping certain purchasing power, balancing, and adjusting life style, expenses, and operating costs back to reality. The key is to correspond according to actual financial situations. When more people are back to work, production and purchases are balanced, leading to a healthy and more stable situation.

Where to have more fund in a recession?

A major problem is finding additional funds in the midst of a recession.

The first method is for people, companies, and the government to have certain levels of savings and inventories, which prepare them for a recession while also avoiding over spending, over production, and over investment during good times. When a recession or other difficulties come, these savings and inventories can be used to overcome them and potential spending. Our current situation is often upside down due to lack of prior savings.

The second method is for unemployed people and companies with financial difficulties to borrow funds with their assets or equalities or to sell partial assets and then allowing them have some time to adjust their life styles or regulate basic production volume and employment back to financially realistic levels. The first two traditional methods are often not possible for some people and companies, who lack savings and assets, which are needed for better future.

The third method is for unemployed people who have difficulties to borrow money, but only up to 80-90% of their own retirement funds in IRA, 401 K, bonds or stocks as equalities including interests under certain regulations from the government, fund management companies or banks. After a recession is over and they once again have normal incomes, they then return their borrowed money plus interests within a certain number of years, such as three years, to avoid the penalty of 10%. When people apply for these loans from their equalities, they need to pay an application fee to cover its processing cost. The government, fund management companies or banks need to hold or transfer 10 % of their retirement funds to related office(s) and up to 80-90 % of the total funds into money market, CD or guarantee accounts, ensuring security until the loans with interests are paid back. In these cases, the up to 80-90% of the funds are still in the market. After their related loans are returned, then the 10% is then returned to these people. Another option is for unemployed people to withdraw up to 80-90 % of their own retirement funds, in which the withdrawn amounts are not in the market, which may affect economic situations.

The forth method is for the government to reduce its operating cost. The saved funds can be used to reduce budget or deficit and help related projects and people with real needs.

The fifth method is for the U.S. government to return partial loans to foreign countries such as China and Japan instead of asking foreign countries to lend us more money, which affects our economic and political situations. For short term, printing more money and raising the national debt limit reasonably is effective way for short-term opportunities. The U.S. government has borrowed too much from foreign countries and overestimated our national ability and capacity. If the borrowing continues and is not corrected, the U.S. would lose its creditability and cause more problems. We wish the printed money is to be used for purchasing purpose from foreign countries, which may improve U.S. economic situation. When foreign countries purchase U.S. products and services with U.S. dollars, our companies can increase production or service and create more jobs, which also reduces our trade unbalances with China and Japan.

The sixth method involves unemployment benefits from the government's unemployment security fund. When employers lay off more employees, they need to pay higher rates to the unemployment security fund as their responsibility to our society. The seventh method is to provide food stamps and Medicaid for basic living needs to the poor with real needs. If this is to be done, certain government regulations are needed such as for personal uses, cost sharing, and necessary items only. The eighth method is for relatives, friends and non-profit organizations to help unemployed people. The ninth method is to provide low-interest loans to unemployed people and college graduates with potential earnings in the future to meet their basic needs. Also these loans require those close to them, who have equalities, to become cosigners for security reason. The tenth method is for the government to provide mini loans to people and college graduates, who are unemployed, to start small businesses with approved business plans.

If the government bails out or has to stimulate funds toward large companies and banks, the purpose is for these companies to lay off less people and allow banks to lend money to those in need. However, after receiving bailout, banks often become much more conservative and careful when they lend money to people and companies during a recession. Potential customers who have reasonably good credit or some equality might not receive loans from banks because the banks increase their standards significantly in a recession. Companies usually reduce their production and employment during a recession because there is a lack of demand. Sale is a major factor that affects company production and employment. After paying off their debts, large public companies and banks like to attract more potential investors. These reasons have contributed to the high unemployment rate of over 9 % and additional house foreclosure in 2011 even after bailout funds and stimulating funds from the U.S. government were given to large companies and banks.

If related companies and banks receive bailout funds, stimulate funds, or low- or no-interest loans from the government, the government supports are connected personally to executive team members through things such as salary reduction and partial personal asset equality to make sure that the supports from tax payers will be returned after the companies and banks return to normal business levels. When small business owners borrow funds from banks, the banks usually require some personal responsibility to make sure loans will be safely returned. The government could decrease corporation tax rate reasonably as a means to encourage companies to keep operations and not to lay off more people.

When there is a lack of funds and low inflation, the government may print more money and raising the national debt for federal government to support companies and people, operation costs, creating more jobs and opportunities as a short-term solution. However, inflation is an important factor. When the economic situation becomes better or is recovering, the government needs to take related amount of money printed back gradually, keeping it off market to balance and control inflation. Otherwise the non-responsible behavior of printing more money will cause more inflation and damage society and country.

Government policy

The government does not create jobs. Instead the government and its workers use taxes from companies and individuals for public jobs and services. The government should reduce costs and increase operating efficiency as much as possible. When the government makes friendly and reasonable policies, they help companies and individuals to create more jobs and opportunities.

During a recession, governments needs to make friendlier policies such as a reasonably low tax rate or tax deductions for companies, which encourages new and existing companies to create new jobs. Having low or no sale tax on food items can help people to keep food expenses low. To companies, who layoff more employments, governments need to increase their unemployment insurance rate, which is used as partial unemployment benefit fund, for their social responsibility. People without employment may start a small business or become self employed. The government also needs to have friendly policies, such as low tax rate or tax deduction for certain period of time, for the unemployed to start small businesses or become self employed. Creating more jobs at different levels helps the recovery of a recession.

It is very important to increase the efficiency of government operations at the lowest cost as possible. The incomes and benefits of government workers should be balanced and stable, comparable to that of private industries. If government workers have higher incomes and better benefits, like the 2 % pension plan with yearly employment, then the more creative and intellectual people would probably want to become government workers. Jobs, opportunities, businesses, and taxes are created by people in private industries for our society and government in the past, present, and future. It seems like there are many successful individuals who would like to become public leaders. Another option is to elect more leaders, who do not want a salary from the government and are content with a lower income and limited benefits. This option may reduce government operating costs and save more taxes in a recession.

This recession has hurt small business greatly. Large companies can lay off employees, reduce production and cost.

Small companies have no leeway to do so. Small business owners have had a much tougher time than CEOs of large companies during this recession. The gap between the upper and lower class has become even more obvious than before. It is essential for low-income and unemployed people to have a certain purchasing power for their basic living needs and for businesses to have basic production levels and services for their employees and customers. A practical concern and problem within companies is lack of purchasing power from consumers, which leads to a lower production rate. A lower production rate makes unemployment rate high, which also reduces people' purchasing power. This circle does not help society to recover from a recession. If potential consumers (people, companies, and governments) have more savings or purchasing power, then the circle mentioned above could be changed to a positive direction. When more jobs are created, they help the recovery of a recession.

After a recession is over and more taxes are collected, the government needs to have more saving for an emergency fund. One of the problems in the government is that there is not enough saving during non-recession time. Therefore when a recession hits, the government incurs more debts, cuts the budget, and needs more taxes, which make the recession even worse.

The government needs to balance internal and import taxes in order to have stable employment, competitive prices, and reasonable protection. An unbalanced import and export affect employment, market, production, sales, profits, and even social stability. When foreign companies reduce their product/service prices by cutting labor costs or getting export refunds from their governments, then we need to increase related import tax rates. Personal expense is usually one of the major costs. Unnecessary costs should be reduced or eliminated. Recessions also generally increase opportunities to invest in real estate and business at low costs. During a recession, foreign investments could be used. A long-term visiting visa may be designed for the special purpose. Companies who use labors in other countries to cut costs should balance the job reduction in the United States by paying oversea income and import taxes. Reasonable, fair, and stable tax rates play important roles in balancing these different factors for the short term as well as the long term.

Small business

Small business is a good way to increase and create employment opportunities. Any person may start a small business. Both small and large companies hire people. The employment rates of small businesses are at about 60%-70% while employment rates of large businesses at 40%-30%. Their rate is almost two to one. Small business is very important in employment. When a recession hits, large companies usually cut production and lay off employees. Large companies generally respond slower to changes in the market. When large company executives do decide to respond to the changing market, they often cut employees in order to keep certain profits for their investors and their own incomes, bonuses, and benefits. Small business owners operate differently. They want their companies to survive and keep good employees. They are more willing to reduce their own incomes and employee's incomes if possible to keep basic production and services because they do not have many other options. Small businesses also constantly look for other possible business opportunities, allowing them to survive and grow.

The operating cost of a small business is usually low. Consultant services usually have very low starting cost. Starting a small business is relatively easy. Many laid off workers have knowledge and experiences in their fields. If they also have a bit of common business knowledge, it is not difficult for them to start a small business. Of course their small businesses should not have legal conflicts with the business of their former employers. It is not easy to keep or grow their business. If more unemployed people begin to start their own businesses, then less people will claim unemployment benefits from the government. It also has the potential to create even more jobs and opportunities in the future as the small business grows and expands.

Although the government does not create jobs, government policies affect the creation of jobs and business opportunities. The government should make convenient application procedures, friendly policies, low fee and reasonable tax for small business. Simplified government documents and tax filling are good for small business. Some non-profit organizations, which have many retired company executives and small business owners and have provided business consulting services for new small business owners, are good resources. For successful business owners and company executives, the government needs to tax them at reasonably high tax rates. If the government taxes them too much then it seems like a "punishment" on their success. If that is the case, then many, including young people, would not want to risk their ideas, time, investments, and energy to start or run a business because it is of greater risk and cost. A reasonably tax rate can be utilized when assets are passed onto next generation. If there are less self motivated people, then the country will go downhill. Friendly and balanced government tax policies promote more investments for more opportunities and donations from the successful people.

Issue and balance

Globalization is a current trend. Each country is at a different position. If the world was under a simple globalization policy, then many commercial products in the United States could not compete with those from other countries because of the higher labor cost and restrictive environmental regulations in the United States. The policy needs to consider employment, product price, protection, profit, and creation. For example, Harley-Davison products are more expensive when compared to other motorcycles because of the quality and additional labor involved. Reasonable protection of the brand with certain import tax rates on similar foreign made motorcycles has made Harley-Davison a well known brand for long time in the United States. We need to balance the globalization policy, offering reasonable protection, and competitiveness for American products. When more jobs are created in new industries, less protection is not as big of an issue. Yet since there is not enough employment or industry in the United States, we need to protect the employment and products reasonably. The purpose is to reduce the unemployment rate for national stability and to increase purchasing power.

Although technology usually costs more, it helps to increase productivity and operating efficiency, which usually results in reduced employment. Employment, technology, and overall cost need to be balanced. For the short and long terms, it is better to balance employment and technology. For example, developing sources of green energy, like solar energy or wind energy, looks good, but there are many technical difficulties that have high costs. The government needs to spend a reasonable amount on such research and development work. If too much cost involves, it can reduce the employment in other related energy areas. Another example is the high speed railroad, which carries a very high cost and has to compete with other transportation methods such as airplane and current train systems. If areas have a large population that will support something like a high speed train system, then it is fine. However, most areas in the United States do not have such large populations, while areas in Japan, China, or Europe do. In the United States, people tend to drive their vehicles for convenience and take airplane for long distance traveling. There are also serious problems related to the land, technology, equipment, manufacturing, and safety. There are already problems supporting the current train and airplane operations because of the limited customers in the United States. If the high speed train were to be another transportation option, it would take away from the already suffering airplane and regular train systems. When unemployment is a problem, the main goal should be to keep and create more jobs. Cost is another factor.

Worker unions play an important role between employers and employees. More incomes and benefits result in an increased membership fee for workers in worker unions. The additional cost to the company results in a greater production cost, which means that the final product will be less competitive, especially when similar products from other countries have a cheap labor cost. If unions push for unreasonably high incomes or benefits for workers, then the products produced or services will be more expensive and unable to compete with similar products or services from other countries. Non-union workers should have the same right to negotiate with employers directly. We need to balance incomes, benefits, costs, and different factors for reducing cost and increasing competitiveness with reasonable protection.

When people are used to certain situations they typically do not want to change, until "forced" to do so. For instance, in Greece the people and government were used to borrowing money and incurring debt. It was no surprise that eventually the country almost went bankrupt. When that happened, the people of Greece had to face the situation head on, starting anew. When people learn from the past, they will then create a better future. Otherwise there is no pressure to change. When we face challenges, we need to change our attitudes and actions for the change. Employment and economic development problems are resolved gradually as people have more jobs, purchasing power, and as the government starts to pay off its debts and loans.

During a recession people often complain that their leaders lack strong leadership and even ability. When leaders misuse the hope of the people to promise impractical things such as more jobs, stimulating funds, and benefits in order to have or keep their leadership positions. After their terms are over, the economic and political situations are usually even worse. Leaders often lack long term vision, leaving behind the troubles to people and future leaders.

When we compare relative operating costs of government, large business, and small business with different factors on a similar or same performance, it is usually the most expensive to run a government and the lowest to run a small business.

Summary

Before a recession, the people, leaders, and government need to be more sensitive to potential crisis. In a normal situation, the government should have reasonable regulations in order to allow companies to reach their peak potential and hire more employees. Emergency funds or savings are needed. When certain signs appear that point to a potential crisis, the government needs to investigate potential economic crimes and punish crimes to protect the national interest as well as the interests of the people.

During a recession, all people, companies, organizations, and the government need to take own responsibilities and work together. Friendly government policies help to create more jobs and stimulate economic development, allowing for recovery from the recession. Patience, wisdom, understanding, and balance are all needed. To create more opportunities and jobs, while reducing costs are very important.

John H. Lee

2. SOCIAL SECURITY BALANCE

Social security payment and recession

Social security is one of the major factors that, effects a recession and long-term planning. If people are seriously worried about their social security payments, which may be not paid after retirement in their future, then they are not confident enough to spend a little bit more to help the economy recover from a recession. The recent recession, which is of greater magnitude than many recessions of the past, has made many people nervous, leading to much less spending during the recession. Many people believe our current social security system will fail. This is already a fact that makes many people bewildered, not knowing how to plan their future retirement. Why the life-time earnings of about 12.4 % of each gross income over 40 to 48 years cannot support social security payments?

It is reported that Social Security will incur about $600 billion in deficits over the next decade, as the economy struggles to recover. Millions of baby boomers are close to the age of retirement. The government social security retirement program has suffered from the struggling economy. It first went into deficit in 2010 and will permanently slip into the red in 2016. Social Security collected $45 billion less in payroll taxes than it paid out in 2011. More than 54 million people received retirement, disabled or survivor benefit payments from the U.S. Social Security in 2010. The average monthly payment was about $1,076, as reported by the nonpartisan Congressional Budget Office in January, 2011 [5-7].

Our current social security payment calculation relates the taxed social security earnings for every year in work history, average indexed monthly earnings (AIME), inflation adjustments, bend points, and primary insurance amounts (PIA) [8]. Each year may have different inflation adjustment. The first bend point is 90%, the second is 32%, and 15% above the second bend point. Bend points are adjusted for inflation. The calculation of PIA is complicated. Almost all people will not want to actually calculate their PIA numbers. When there are more non-retired working people and more earnings, social security payments shall not have a problem because there is enough earnings. When there are not enough non-retired working people and earnings, social security payments are in a serious problem, which is our situation currently and in next period of time. "Your estimated benefits are based on current law. Congress has made changes to the law in the past and can do so at any time" is often on individual Social Security statements. The current situation needs to be improved to avoid a fallout. Can it be done by balancing social security earnings and payments?

Many countries like the United States, Japan, China, France, and Greece face or will face the same problem as more people enter the retirement age and there are not enough working people and social security earnings to support the retired and disabled people. When the French government did not have enough funds to support its retirees and it increased the minimum retirement age from 60 to 62 and the age to receive full government benefits from 65 to 67 in 2010, there were many significant demonstrations against the changes [9]. Most people would like to make sure that their social security earnings from their working years will be there as social security payments when they retire. Another issue is that some people are not responsible and want to work less and get more. Are governments or people responsible for that situation and shortage problem? Letting people know how much their own social security earnings (from employees and employers) including compounded interest from their working years will result in people having more respect for their own social security earnings and payments. If people were to receive social security payments according to their own earnings, there would be more social stability.

Most people need to be responsible for themselves, saving enough, including their own social security earnings, during their working years for social security payments during their retirements. The government should not need to take the responsibility of social security earnings away from people. If so, then the government will have either more power when there is enough social security earnings, or more trouble when there is not enough social security payments. More power means that it may be easy for the government and government officers to use a part of social security earnings for non-related people or projects.

Social security earnings and payment are the two sides, which need to be balanced. If we have more and more receivers for payments, there are no enough social security earnings to support, which breaks the balance. Then problems such as financial shortage will come because of not enough savings and social security earnings. The Greek situations for the government to borrow money almost caused their national bankruptcy in 2010. What can we learn from these situations in the United States, France, Greece, and other countries?

Many people know that if they continue their purchases, it will contribute to our society and reduce a recession gradually. If people know and believe they would have their social security payments from their own earnings without fail in the future, people will feel much more confident to spend a little bit more and to help recovering from a recession.

Social security earning and payment

Most people begin to work at age 18 to 22 after high schools or colleges. The current age to receive full retirement benefits in the United States is raised from 65 to 67 years old. So people usually work for 40 to 48 years before retirement, which means employees and employers save about 12.4 % (6.2x2 %) of gross income for 40 to 48 years from each paycheck. How much total social security earnings will be? Are these earnings plus other personal IRA, 401K, savings, and assets enough for retired people?

When a couple with an average annual income of $60,000/year (or each spouse has average annual income at $30,000/year), which is a typical mid-income family, and employment from 18-22 to 65-67 years old (assuming 40 years) at 6.2 x 2 % with a compounded annual interest 3 %, their total social security earnings is $574,156, in which the net earnings is $297,600 (60,000 x 6.2 % x 2 x 40) at $310x2/month. Net social security earnings is usually provided by individual social security statements. If $574,156 is divided over 15 years with a compounded annual interest 3%, its social security payment is $3,965/month or $47,580/year from 67 to 82. If $574,156 is divided over 20 years with 3% interest, its social security payment is $3,184/month or $38,208/year from 67 to 87. Social security payments plus other personal IRA, 401K, savings, and assets can be used to cover food, utilities, insurance, and other expenses during their retirements. The life expectancy at birth in the United States was 78.3 in 2010. The life expectancy projection in 2020 is 79.5.

For a life term, no matter how long people live, annuity payment is currently often simplified over 20 years according to total contributions at the retirement age of 67 years old by financial service calculations. Some people live longer and some shorter. Life expectancy projection and inflation are considered as major factors. Other factors are simply neglected. When life expectancy increases gradually, situations may be changed. The U.S. life expectancy at birth and projections from 1970 to 2020 are: 70.8 years old (1970), 73.7 (1980), 75.4 (1990), 76.8 (2000), 77.4 (2005), 78.3 (2010), 78.9 (2015) and 79.5 (2020). There are some data about life expectancy at age 65 and 75. The Social Security Administration shows U.S. life expectancy at age 65. A man reaching age 65 now can expect to live to 83 on average. A woman turning age 65 today can expect to live to 85 on average [10-12]. Life expectancy at age 67 and projections, which are needed, may be used for more accurate calculations.

If a working person has annual income $20,000, which is low income, his or her social security tax is $103.33/month at 6.2 %. The person will have total social security earnings about $191,385 after working 40 years with a compounded annual interest 3 %, in which the net earnings is $99,200 (20,000 x 6.2 % x 2 x 40) at $103x2/month. If $191,385 is divided over 15 years with 3% annual interest, his or her social security payment is $1,322/month or $15,860/year. These data can be found in Tables 1, 2 and 3.

If a working person has annual income $45,000, his or her social security tax is $232.50/month at 6.2 %, which is a typical low-mid income. The person will have total social security earnings about $430,617 after working for 40 years with a compounded annual interest 3 %, in which the net earnings is $223,200 (45,000 x 6.2 % x 2 x 40). If $430,617 is divided over 20 years with 3% annual interest, his or her social security payment is $2,388/month or $28,658/year.

When reaching retirement ages, most retired people have paid most or all of home mortgages. Living costs for clothes, foods, goods, and activities are reduced compared with the situations before retirement. Medical expense and travel cost are usually increased. For a single person, the 2009/2010 poverty level was $10,830 /year. For a family of two, the poverty level was $14,570/year [1], based on a calculation that includes only cash income, before tax deductions, which are shown in Table 4. Most people have additional retirement funds from such as 401K, IRA, personal savings, and housing change (from large house down to small house or apartment).

How much can we have in total social security earnings over 30 to 45 years? When a person has $100/month for social security tax, then the total earnings over 40 years will be $185,212 at compounded annual interest 3 % or $305,204 at compounded annual interest 5 %. When a person has $500/month for social security tax, then the total earnings over 40 years will be $926,059 at compounded annual interest 3 % or $1,526,020 at compounded annual interest 5 %. Total value of social security earnings over 30 to 45 years at compounded annual interest 3% or 5% is shown by Tables 1 and 2. Social security tax at a few hundred dollars per month could produce a large amount of earnings over 30 to 45 years.

Table 1 Total value after 30-45 years (annual interest 3 %)

By employee	Total value by employee and employer's match			
$/month\Years	30	35	40	45
50	58,274	74,156	92,606	114,037
100	116,548	148,312	185,212	228,074
200	233,096	296,624	370,424	456,148
300	349,644	444,936	555,636	684,222
400	466192	593,248	740,848	912,296
500	582,736	741,563	926,059	1,140,372

Table 2 Total value after 30-45 years (annual interest 5 %)

By employee	Total value by employee and employer's match			
$/month\Years	30	35	40	45
50	83,226	113,609	152,602	202,644
100	166,452	227,218	305,204	405,288
200	332,904	454,436	610,208	810,576
300	499,356	681,654	915,612	1,215,864
400	665,808	908,872	1,220,416	1,621,152
500	832,258	1,136,092	1,526,020	2,026,437

Table 3 Monthly payment for 10-25 years (annual interest 3 %/y)

Total $ \ Years	10	15	20	25
100,000	966	691	555	474
200,000	1,931	1,381	1,109	948
300,000	2,897	2,072	1,664	1,422
400,000	3,862	2,762	2,218	1,896
500,000	4,828	3,453	2,773	2,371
600,000	5,793	4,143	3,328	2,845
700,000	6,759	4,834	3,882	3,319
800,000	7,724	5,524	4,437	3,794
900,000	8,690	6,215	4,992	4,268
1,000,000	9,656	6,906	5,546	4,742
1,200,000	11,587	8,287	6,655	5,690
1,400,000	13,518	9,668	7,763	6,639
1,600,000	15,449	11,050	8,874	7,587
1,800,000	17,380	12,431	9,982	8,536
2,000,000	19,312	13,812	11,092	9,484

Total value of social security earnings is then withdrawn during retirement from the age 67 normally. Table 3 shows monthly benefit payments from total earnings of $100,000 to $2,000,000 over 10 to 25 years. When $200,000 is withdrawn over 15 years with 3% interest, its annuity benefit payment is $1,381/month or $16,572/year. When $600,000 is withdrawn over 15 years with 3% interest, its annuity payment is $4,143/month or $49,716/year, which may already be more than a Social Security maximum payment.

Table 4   2009/2010 Poverty Guidelines ($/ year)

Size of family	1	2	3	4
Poverty ($)	10,830	14,570	18,310	22,050
120 %	12,996	17,484	21,972	26,460
150 %	16,245	21,855	27,465	33,075
200 %	21,660	29,140	36,620	44,100

"Self-Support" system without fail

Can we build a practical "Self-Support" system for social security to balance earnings and benefit payments? If yes, the system will not fail. We need to consider both how much social security earnings we have and how much payments we can pay for each and all retired people and to have their balance at the same time.

The social security earnings by 12.4 % (6.2x2 %) of gross income over 40 to 48 years, for most people, usually is a nice saving. The principle is to let most people to take care of their own social security and balance their earnings and payments. "Self" means for most people to be responsible for their own social security payments after their retirement by their own social security earnings and employers' matches. "Support" means to allocate partial social security earnings from mid- to high-income people and their employers' matches over a maximum retirement payment to help old poor and disabled people with real needs. All sources of 401 K, IRA, personal savings, social security payments, and additional social security payment are added together to reach a minimum retirement payment, which may be such as 85% or 100% of poverty line to cover very basic living expenses. Survivor (children under 18 and retired spouse) benefits are from employees' own earnings after considering age, incomes, marriage length, and shares if having more than one marriage. Additional social security help is provided as possible if retired people have below certain poverty line. Maximum social security benefit payment may be such as 200% or 250% of poverty line. The reasonable government management cost is another factor. Banks usually provide free services for depositors. Non-load mutual fund management companies usually charge for their service fees at 0.5 to 1 %.

People in our society agree that high-income people shall contribute more, low-income people contribute less and we should help elderly poor and disabled people with real needs. Also disabled and poor people need to do their best. Our policies should make people to be more responsible and not depend on help from governments as possible. This will also affect young people. If more people do not take own responsibility and depend on help from governments for long term, then poverty problems will not be reduced and resolved.

Related numbers such as how much are related minimum and maximum social security benefit payments, retirement age, up to salary amount, and rate shall be professional issues instead of political problems, which shall be provided by economists instead of politicians after balancing social security earnings and benefit payments.

The federal government may inject certain operation funds, which shall be stable over time. Then the "Self-Support" social security system will not be affected by non-retired working people's social security earnings and economic situations. The "Self-Support" system will pay retirement payments fairly by people's own earnings and help elderly poor and disabled people with practical and reasonable payments without fail, which also will help young people to learn to be responsible for their own future and support their society.

Calculation and balance

There are two balances for each and all retired people between social security earnings and retirement benefit payments. If a retired person has equal or more than a maximum social security payment, then the person is paid with the maximum payment. If a retired person has less than maximum social security payment, the person is paid by own social security earnings. There are three groups of retired people. In the Group #1, retired people are paid by a maximum social security payment. In the Group #2, retired people are paid by their own social security earnings. In the Group #3, elderly poor and disabled people with real needs may apply for up to a minimum social security payment. Each retired person has own social security earning balance.

For Group #1:

TE/PA*C > or = Max P: Social security payment = Max P

TE: total social security earnings including compounded annual interest from employee and employer(s) when an elderly person applies for social security payment;
PA: projected life expectancy subtracts retied age;
C: adjustable number after considering inflation, life expectancy increase over time, and others, which may be different or constant each year and
Max P: maximum social security payment, which may be such as 200% of poverty line.

If we set 200% of current poverty line at $21,660/year or $1805/month as a maximum social security payment and PA*C at 20 years (or 240 months), a person needs total social security earnings of $325,500 with a compounded annual interest 3 %. It means the person needs to contribute $175.75/month for 40 years with a compounded annual interest 3 %, in which the person has annual income $34,016 or $2,835/month. The amount of 6.2 % x \$2,835/month is \$175.75/month. Many people have more than the annual income \$34,016, which means they can have the maximum social security payment \$1805/month. Their extra parts could be used for helping elderly poor and disabled people with real needs.

When adding all extra amounts over Max P together, we can know their total amount, which can be used for help at certain year or a period of time. Adjusting Max P payment affects the total extra amount. We need to adjust reasonable Max P payment to have its balance with Group #3.

For Group #2:

TE/PA*C < Max P: Social security payment = TE/PA*C

Except Group #1, all left retired people are in this Group #2. Non-working spouses may share their spouses' left balances from employees' earnings.

For Group #3:

Poor elderly and disabled people and survivors with low income and asset may apply for their additional social security payments to meet a minimum social security payment after deducting their combinations of their own social security earnings, personal 401 K, IRA, assets, properties, and savings. In their applications, a reasonable application fee is needed, which may be waived if there are certain difficulties. It needs to be prevented for some applicants to apply for additional social security payment after transferring their assets to their children, relatives and friends or hiding their assets. When retired people have children, their children's emotional and financial supports are also important.

Additional social security payment = Min P - OE - OP

Min P: minimum payment;
OE: own social security earnings over PA*C and
OP: all own personal 401 K, IRA, assets, properties, and savings over PA*C

When adding all additional social security payments together, we can know their total amount, which is needed for poor and disabled people and survivors. Adjusting Min P payment affects total amount. When we decrease Min P payment, there will be less needed. When we increase Min P payment, there will be more needed. We need to set or adjust reasonable Min P payment.

Group #1 and Group #3 are needed to be balanced for certain year or a period of time.

$$\sum_{n=1}^{n} (TE/PA*C-Max\ P)+G = or > \sum_{m=1}^{m} (Min\ P-OE-OP) \ ......(1)$$

G: government contribution (+), management fee (-), prior balance, and adjustment;

The left side of the above equation (1) of SUM (TE/PA*C - Max P) + G means total extra social security fund amount available, which can be increased by decreasing Max P and increasing G. The right side of the above equation of SUM (Min P - OE - OP) means total additional social security payment amount needed, which can be decreased by decreasing Min P and increasing OE and OP. The right side number shall be less or equal to the left side number. We need to think practical and professional considerations to balance this equation instead of political concerns.

A computer program for the above calculations of the groups #1, #2 and #3 may be designed. The equation (1) may be balanced professionally by adjusting these different factors.

If we set $21,660/year or $1805/month, which is 200% of poverty line in 2009/2010 as a maximum payment and PA*C is 20, then all extra contributions over the income $34,016/year or $2,835/month can be used for helping old poor and disabled people and survivors with real needs.

Table 5 shows the U.S. family income distribution (%) in 2008 according to www.census.gov [13, 14]. Family annual income below $20,000/year was 12.1%. Family income between $20,000 to $100,000/year was 61.9%. Family income above $100,000/year was 26.0%.

Table 5 The U.S. family income distribution (%) in 2008 (all races)

Income interval	Number of families (1,000)	Percent distribution
All families	78,874	100.0
Under $10,000	3,787	4.8
$10,000 to $14,999	2,584	3.3
$15,000 to $19,999	3,175	4.0
$20,000 to $24,999	3,932	5.0
$25,000 to $29,999	3,798	4.8
$30,000 to $34,999	3,858	4.9
$35,000 to $39,999	3,774	4.8
$40,000 to $44,999	3,715	4.7
$45,000 to $49,999	3,242	4.1
$50,000 to $59,999	6,395	8.1
$60,000 to $74,999	8,872	11.2
$75,000 to $84,999	5,137	6.5
$85,000 to $99,999	6,115	7.8
$100,000 to $149,999	11,967	15.2
$150,000 to $199,999	4,561	5.8
$200,000 to $249,999	1,726	2.2
$250,000 and above	2,230	2.8

John H. Lee

When people know their own social security earnings, they can calculate their own social security benefit payments after retirement. Then people will feel more confident, know how to arrange and plan their life expenses with their own social security earnings and personal savings, 401 K, IRA, and assets. Detail information helps people to make plans and be confident financially and emotionally, which contribute to our society and minimize a recession and result in quicker recovery.

For most people, total social security earnings is equal or more than total benefit payments during retirement. When a retired person dies, left partial social security earnings may be paid to his or her qualified survivor or contributed to the factor G in the above equation (1), which may be used to help poor retired and disabled people. Of course some people live longer than PA*C together, they would receive more social security benefit payments than own earnings. After withdrawing all their own social security earnings, their social security benefit payments are from others. They may belong to the Group #3. Life-term benefit payments are provided to all retired people.

We can start the "Self-Support" social security system for young people or all people anytime after enough preparations. Here are the procedures to deal with actual situations:

1. To figure out total personal social security earnings including compounded interest before starting retirement or current balances after deducting social security payments already received by retired people;
2. To set and adjust to reasonable minimum and maximum social security payments, PA, C factor, G factors, and equation (1) and
3. To balance all calculations for Groups #1, 2 and 3.

During a recession, payroll social security tax reduction is often used for employees to have more money to be spent, which helps to recover a recession. It was reported that the

36

Senate approved a $1 trillion bill to fund the government and a two-month extension of the payroll social security tax reduction 2% for 2012 on December 17, 2011 (Saturday). Then Democrats and Republicans argued and finally agreed to extend payroll social security tax reduction 2% for the left ten months in February, 2012 [15]. With the "Self-Support" social security system, the payroll social security tax reduction does not need to be supported by any government fund. Each and all people are supported by own social security earnings, responsible for their social security payments and balance the equation (1). If government fund such as $500 billion is borrowed into the "Self- Support" social security system, the fund is stable for its operation over time if not spent.

If there is certain shortage in our social security payments, their balances from the equation (1) may be calculated, balanced, and matched. For example if there is $100 billion short this year, the equation (1) may be adjusted and balanced over next period of time such as to 10 years. If about 50 million people receive social security payments, then the factor G includes the adjustment -$10 billion/year to reach its final balance after 10 years by adjusting these factors. If the $10 billion is divided by 50 million people, each will receive less $200/year (or $17/month).

$$\sum_{n=1}^{n} (TE/PA*C\text{-Max } P)+(G-10 \times 10^9)=\sum_{m=1}^{m} (\text{Min P-OE-OP}) \dots (2)$$

If there is more positive balance (PB) left in our social security system, the PB may be reserved for future use.

$$\sum_{n=1}^{n} (TE/PA*C\text{-Max } P)+G - \sum_{m=1}^{m} (\text{Min P-OE-OP}) = PB \dots\dots (3)$$

There are different proposals such as to allow younger workers to build their social security plans to bypass Social Security and choose private investment companies because the current Social Security program already shown in fail. The private investment proposals are similar as 401K programs with different rates. The serious problem may happen in the future. What can we do if there are more younger workers like to have more spending instead of depositing social security tax for their future? For example most companies provide matching programs at 3 to 5% for 401K to their employees. Some younger workers give up 401K until they are 30 or 40's. We may use the "Self-Support" social security system without fail.

Issue

For social security system, we need to deal with serious questions and issues such as:

(1) Are social security earnings over 40-48 years to most people enough for their own retirement payments?
(2) If social security earnings for most people (such as 90%) are not enough, it needs to increase its rate.
(3) Increasing minimum working years from 10 years to 15 years to be qualified may increase social security earnings.
(4) Adjust maximum and minimum social security benefit payments to have their balance and
(5) To have balance between social security earnings and payments after considering different factors.

When social security earnings for most people are not enough, it is good way to increase social security rate for more earnings from the current 6.2 % to 6.5%, 6.7% or 7% (Table 6); When social security for old poor and disabled people is not enough, to reduce maximum social security payment slightly, increase up to salary amount from $106,800 to such as $110,000 or $120,000, or/and reduce minimum social security payment slightly may be good ways. Another factor is people's life expectancy, which increases gradually. Inflation is an important factor. More inflation will decrease values of total social security earnings and increase needs of social security payments.

Table 6 Monthly S.S. tax by employee's contribution

Income/M	6.2%	6.5%	6.7%	7.0%
1,000	62	65	67	70
2,000	124	130	134	140
3,000	186	195	201	210
4,000	248	260	268	280
5,000	310	325	335	350
6,000	372	390	402	420
7,000	434	455	469	490
8,000	496	520	536	560
9,000	558	585	603	630
10,000	620	650	670	700

Some people suggest if anyone makes more than $100,000 a year during retirement, he or she should not receive any social security benefit payment because our social security system does not have enough funds. If there is no significant shortage, we shall have fair policy and treat different people equally to have social security payments from own earnings although high-income people have extra social security earnings more than a social security maximum payment. The government shall send them "Thank You" note for their contributions every year.

From above calculations and data tables, most people shall have enough social security earnings to be responsible to their own social security payments for their retirement. If there are no enough social security funds, we need to increase social security tax rate, up to amount of income taxed, yearly eligibility, and adjust minimum and maximum social security payments to meet our needs. These issues should be done in a professional way to balance social security earnings and payments instead of political way. Any political way may create more problems and not use social resources properly. The "Self-Support" system for our social security will work without fail.

3. EDUCATION AND HEALTH CARE

Education goal and balance

We all know that training our children to have knowledge, self management, good health, creativity, good attitude, good value, responsibility, good relationship, confidence, critical thinking, respect, and balance is very important.

There are two extreme sides to raising kids. One is to let children do whatever they want. Children need to figure out everything for themselves. Some of these children end up have no goals in life and do not know what to do. The other side of the spectrum is overprotective parents who do almost everything for their kids. They allow their children almost no free time to think or enjoy things like video games, T.V., sports or crafts. Amy Chua describes her type of method in her book Battle Hymn of the Tiger Mother, which has become a hot topic in the United States. Some parents and teachers support her method while others don't. Parents and teachers need to give children proper instructions. Yet children also need to have their fun and free time. Children and parents need to learn to balance their time, to be responsible, and to manage their spending habits and behaviors. Better living conditions are good for children, which also often make children less responsible, thinking less about the future and spending an increased amount of time playing video games and watching TV if parents and teachers do not pay attention. The children who come from better living conditions often do less because they think there is nothing that they need to concern. Parents and schools need to provide opportunities to train children to be responsible and independent with self control and management. Self management is a major factor for children to be successful, which needs long-time training. Overspending is a significant social problem that children from better living conditions to face. We need to teach students to balance their earnings, expenses, donations, and savings.

Our society needs doctors, lawyers, engineers, designers, and teachers. We also need technicians, manufacturing workers, construction laborers, skilled workers, and farmers. A society needs to have a balance of different people, majors, and industries. All of them are important to our society. In some countries, most high school students go to college for the bachelors, masters, or even PhD degrees. It looks good. Also education standards are often reduced to reach the goal. Yet when many of these college students graduate they cannot find related jobs, which cause serious problems in that society.

Education is one of major social costs. The government provides basic elementary, middle, and high school education for students. The cost of public education poses a significant challenge. The government may require more personal responsibility and provide more cost sharing, reasonable students loans, and less grants to reduce related costs as possible and provide more opportunities to students as well as more responsibilities. Students and parents need to balance their personal interests, financial availability, academic pursuits, and jobs. Students need to learn to be responsible for themselves, their families, and society. Training students to become good citizens is important. Students often need to check the "who, what, where, when, and why (5Ws) of their situations. We should do our best to have right motivations and processes and not be overly concerned with results because there are usually too many factors that beyond our control.

Of course our society needs to give young people more and equal opportunities. Young people, who are the same as adults, are different each other. Some of them are good in such as playing sports, studying science, liking number-related work or people-related work. We need to let them to develop their potentials and take responsibilities. Such as their race, religion, nationality, and background should not be considered as related factors for their equal rights. Otherwise discrimination by race, religion, nationality, and background may be created against equal opportunities and rights. We need to treat everybody as an individual to avoid racial, religious, and political issues and potential conflicts. College admission standards such as knowledge, skill, social service, leadership, and talent factors are the same for all students. When students have special talents, college may add their talents for additional considerations, which are not based on their race, religion, nationality, and background. Also for college sport teams to choice their team members uses the same standards such as skill, physical condition, and team work, which should not connected to non-related factors such as by race, religion, nationality, and background. Of course we need to balance different factors for equal right and non-discrimination environment.

After graduating high school, students should be able to find jobs or start their own small business, living a reasonable quality of life. College graduates should also be able to find jobs and live with a certain quality of life while returning student loans. We need to keep low inflation and lower basic living costs (food, rent, utilities, and basic medical insurance/services) as possible. If we do so, then living costs would not be a problem for young people after they graduate from high school or college and enter real society.

To have a business is a dream for many people, especially young people. Many entrepreneurs start their businesses at a young age. Young people have a greater passion to become entrepreneurs. Of course experiences also play an important role. Mature ideas, investments, actions, operations, innovations, and management make entrepreneurs more successful. Only a portion of entrepreneurs can survive after five or ten years of operations. Businesses create jobs not only for the business owners but also for many other people.

We spend more money in public education than many other countries. Public schooling costs increase over time. Teachers need to have competitive salaries in order to be able to focus on teaching children. Public schools could reduce operation costs through different areas such as utility reduction, after school activities or services, and increases building usage on nights and weekends to such as rent to adult training colleges and churches. Teacher unions play an important role in the balancing of teachers' incomes/benefits and teaching responsibilities. In the past when the teachers' unions negotiated with school districts, schools would close because teachers would not teach. Our goal should be to put children and their education first.

It is a challenge to train students to have good knowledge, self management, good attitudes, responsibility, and balanced life at reasonable cost. Students, parents, teachers, schools, society, and the government need to work together.

Steve and Stacy had a 15-year old son, Kevin. They required Kevin to work 7 to 10 hours per week after school and more than 10 hours per week during summer vacation. Working too much would affect his school work. By working Kevin made money of his own and avoided spending too much time on video games and television. Kevin was allowed to spend up to 50% of his earnings. The rest was saved for college expenses. Kevin graduated high school with honors and also had $3,870 in his bank. Kevin then went to a local university, majoring in engineering. His parents still required him to work 25 to 40 hours per month during the semester and more during break. Kevin's parents matched his earnings at 2:1 up to 40 hours/month and required him to record his earnings and expenses. Steve and Stacy paid Kevin's tuition, medical insurance, rent, computer, car, and basic fees. However they required Kevin to take care of his own food, clothe, phone, internet, utilities, gasoline, books, and repairs with the money he earned from his work and parents. They also set an emergency fund of $5,000 for Kevin and told him that the fund was available when he had difficulties and he was welcome to back home anytime. During his four years at college, Kevin did not use the emergency fund at all. After four years, Kevin graduated from his university with honors and an overall GPA 3.6. He also found an engineer job in a local company.

Health care issue

Health care is another major cost. The health care bill was signed into the law in 2010, which divided Americans, especially Democrats and Republicans. We need to ask whether this law will work well for the long term. If it costs too much, then in the long term it is not practical. Even if the bill looks "nice", if it does not work well then we will have an even greater budget shortage and increase the national debt. Patients will then have to wait for a long time for necessary medical treatments and operations because of the budget shortage, in which related government officers then may have related corruption. When a large medical system is damaged, then it will affect so many people. In the current medical service, patients usually have full right to pick their own doctors, hospitals, and special medical providers. Another way is that patients have limited right to pick their doctors and hospitals, which is more similar to "mass production". Then their costs may be reduced. We may need different medical services to meet patient needs at different costs.

Health care costs are interesting. When more people balance their life physically, economically, and psychologically, more people have better health, meaning less obesity and diseases, which will reduce health care costs significantly. If more people have heath issues such as diabetes, obesity, high blood pressure, eating disorders, or heart disease, then health care costs will be increased significantly.

We do need to provide basic health care including emergency medical services for the poor and the disabled with real needs at reasonable and competitive costs. Certain governmental policies are needed for these recipients, medical providers, and medical insurance companies. These recipients also need to follow certain instructions and regulations to improve their situations as possible, which directly relate to their diseases such as reducing their overweight or stopping smoking habit. Serious diseases, such as HIV, are mainly caused and transferred by sexual intercourse and blood transfusions. Currently there are many HIV cases in many countries. If the annual treatment cost for a HIV patient is such as $30,000, who is responsible? When related tests are done before blood transfer and sexual intercourse, then related diseases by blood transfusions and sexual activities can be reduced significantly. When individuals manage and consider their sexual actions seriously, then HIV and many sexual diseases can be controlled and reduced significantly.

In Philippine, it was reported that at least 46 % of HIV infections recorded in 2010 were from heterosexual contact compared to the 25 % in 2006, according to the government data. Previously, HIV had been mainly spread through homosexual contact. Needle injection is considered as another major method of the infection. The Center for Diseases Control and Prevention (CDC) estimates that 1.2 million people in the United States are living with HIV infection, in which 20% (one of five) of those people with HIV are unaware of their infection. The U.N. and W.H.O. figures estimate there were approximately 34 million people living with HIV in 2010. Millions of people are afraid to be tested because of the fear associated with HIV [16-18]. HIV is one of the world's leading infectious killers.

Emergency medical service is an important and critical area for people without medical insurance to use emergency medical service and do not pay. If it is not properly handled, the emergency medical service may go bankrupt. Some emergency medical services have been shut down because it is very costly and some people do not pay back debts. Because of this all people are facing the serious problem with emergency medical services. For emergency medical service fees, there are different rates. One is for people with insurances from insurance companies or the government. Another is for people without insurance. We need to require or provide people basic emergency medical services that also require personal responsibility at the same time.

Patients and their families often complain about high price of medical and hospital services. Hospitals and doctors often complain high cost of doctors' insurance and lawsuits against doctors and hospitals from patients and their families besides some patients without medical insurance and do not pay debts. Attorneys often help related patients and share a rate such as 30% after they win without direct charge, in which patients and their families prefer to do without any payment. All costs including unpaid emergency medical services and lawsuit charges are transferred to these patients, who pay their medical bills, and make medical cost so expensive.

Peter was a small business owner. He, his wife and their son purchased their medical insurance for more than twenty years. One night Peter felt a heavy pressure around his heart and had trouble breathing. His wife sent him to a hospital emergency room. Doctors found blood clots in his heart. They gave him and his wife two options, to treat the clots which would cost about ten thousand dollars or to have heart surgery which would cost more than two hundred thousand dollars. The second option was too expensive, even with the insurance company sharing the cost, and so they chose the first option. After having the small operation, Peter took medicine and did not go to work for two months. Their insurance company also increased their insurance price. Then his situation was stable and he eventually returned to work. After six months when he was home alone he had a heart attack. When his wife and their son returned home, they found his body and called 911. He passed away at the age of 49.

Ron worked in a company as a labor contractor. He had no medical insurance coverage, thinking medical insurance was too expensive. One morning, he felt pressure around his chest and proceeded to go to the emergency room. Doctors found there was blood clots in his heart and suggested he to have heart surgery. After two days, the doctors did the operation that cost about two hundred fifty thousand dollars. He owned a middle-class house and some savings. His annual income was not high. Ron claimed low income and then almost all medical expenses were waived. He had no any heart problems even after five years.

There is the significant argument. One side is to support requiring citizens to buy medical insurance. Even the government likes to mandate citizens to buy medical insurance. Another side is to let citizens to have their right and freedom to choice and government cannot mandate citizens to buy medical insurance. The governmental mandate is against our Constitution. Both sides have their reasons and are right. But there will be serious problems if we do not handle both sides properly. The best is to balance them together. Yes, citizens have their freedom and right to buy medical insurance. If a person does not buy medical insurance, uses emergency medical service in a hospital, and does not pay, then tax payers and public need to pay his or her cost. For Ron's case, his local government or donators usually need to pay or otherwise the hospital would go to bankruptcy if there are more cases. When citizens are required to have basic medical insurance at least to cover such as emergency medical service, then tax payers, public, and governments do not need to pay related medical expenses for people, who have emergency medical service. When citizens' freedom and options affect public safety or significant concerns, then these issues become more complex, which need to be balanced with some regulations. For example vehicle insurance, which is considered as a similar situation, drivers are required to buy liability insurance at least to cover any potential accident. Beyond basic liability insurance, citizens have their right and freedom to buy more coverage or not.

For people or elderly people with incurable diseases, facing death positively is very important. Positive attitudes are helpful for people to face and overcome the fear of death, difficulties, life problems, and financial shortages without or with less depression. Individuals, medical providers, medical insurance companies, employers, and the government need to work together and take own responsibilities. Everybody will face death. Death and near-death experiences are discussed in Chapter 8.

"Self-Support" Medicare

Medicare for the retired is another major social cost. Is it possible to build another practical "Self-Support" Medicare system, which is similar to "Self-Support" social security system, so that Medicare can balance between earnings and payments? If so, then the system will not fail.

When a couple with an average annual income of $60,000/year, which is a typically mid income family, is employed from the age of about 18-22 to 65-67 (assuming 40 years) with a compounded annual interest of 3%, their total Medicare earning is $134,278.5 from both employee and employer. The net Medicare earning is $69,600 (1.45%x2x60,000x40) with the monthly earning at $72.5x2 (1.45%x2x60,000/12). If the total Medicare earning is divided over 15 years with 3% interest, the payments are $927/month (or $11,124/year), which can be used as the benefit for purchasing Medicare. Table 7 shows the total Medicare earnings from each monthly Medicare tax after 30-45 years. Table 8 shows monthly Medicare payments from total Medicare earnings over 10-25 years.

Table 7 Total value after 30-45 years (annual interest 3 %)

By employee $/month \ Years	Total value by employee and employer's match			
	30	35	40	45
10	11,655	14,831	18,321	22,807
20	23,309	29,662	36,642	45,614
50	58,273	74,156	92,606	114,037
70	81,585	103,817	128,247	159,649
100	116,546	148,312	183,212	228,072
120	139,860	177,972	219,852	273,684
150	174,825	222,465	274,815	342,105

Table 8 Monthly payments for 10-25 years (interest 3 %/y)

Total $ \ Years	10	15	20	25
20,000	193	138	111	95
50,000	483	345	277	237
100,000	966	691	555	474
200,000	1,931	1,381	1,109	948
300,000	2,897	2,072	1,664	1,423
400,000	3,862	2,762	2,218	1,897

The federal government provides billions of dollars to Medicare. The current Medicare has the four programs. Most people age 65 or older who are citizens or permanent residents of the United States are eligible for free Medicare hospital insurance (Part A). Anyone who is eligible for free Medicare hospital insurance (Part A) can enroll in Medicare medical insurance (Part B) by paying a monthly premium. For Medicare Advantage plans (Part C), if persons have Medicare Parts A and B, the persons can join the Medicare Advantage plan. Medicare Advantage plans are offered by private companies and approved by Medicare. The participators might have to pay a monthly premium for Medicare Advantage plan because of the extra benefits it offers. For Medicare prescription drug plans (Part D), anyone who has Medicare hospital insurance (Part A), medical insurance (Part B) or a Medicare Advantage plan (Part C) is eligible for prescription drug coverage (Part D). Joining a Medicare prescription drug plan is voluntary, and need to pay an additional monthly premium for the coverage. Some beneficiaries with higher incomes will pay a higher monthly Part D premium [19].

Only Medicare hospital insurance (Part A) is free for qualified people. Parts B, C and D need people to pay monthly premiums. People and their employers pay Medicare taxes at $1.45 \times 2\%$ over time during their working years. We need to increase personal responsibility and government efficiency and transparency to avoid transferring Medicare taxes to other uses. If there is not enough contributions, rates and other factors may be adjusted to meet Medicare needs, which are similar to social security earnings and payments. The principle is slightly different from the "Self-Support" social security system. We need to consider both what we can do and what we should do at the same time and have them to be balanced. This way the "Self-Support" Medicare system will not fail.

We may let partial Medicare taxes such as 50% of total amount of all Medicare taxes to pay a basic Medicare program A for all qualified retired people. Partial amount such as 30% is returned to retired people as Medicare benefit payments by their own Medicare earnings to purchase additional Medicare programs or medical expenses beyond basic Medicare program A. The left is used for the government to pay Medicare expenses. We need to balance Medicare taxes and payments.

Medicare taxes may be divided into three parts. In the Part #1, a portion such as 50% of total Medicare taxes from all retired people at certain year is used to cover all qualified retired people including their non-working spouses for a basic Medicare program A including (1) basic medical insurance; (2) basic hospital insurance, and (3) basic prescription drug coverage. Basic emergency service and regular physical examination are included. There are reasonable deductable such as $3,000/year and expense sharing such as 20%:80% within network doctor services or 30%:70% without network doctor services after the deductable. Actual coverage depends on the amount from the equation (4).

Part #1:

$$\sum_{p=1}^{p} (50\%*TME/PA*C)+G)/p = \text{each retied person's amount} \quad .....(4)$$

TME: total personal Medicare earnings plus interest;
PA: projected life expectancy subtracts retired age;
C: adjustable number after considering inflation, life expectancy increase over time, and other major factors;
G: government tax support (+), management fee (-), prior balance and adjustment and
p: total number for all qualified retired people including their qualified non-working spouses.

For non-qualified retied people such as legal retired immigrants, they or their financial sponsors may pay related Medicare premium without government support.

$$\sum_{p=1}^{p}(50\%*TME/PA*C)/p*F = \text{for non-qualified retied person} \quad ...(5)$$

F is an adjustable factor.

There are also other Medicare programs B, C, or D with better coverage, which can be purchased by additional payments.

Part #2:

Each qualified retired person can receive a percentage such as 30%*TME over PA*C per year if they did not exceed a maximum Medicare payment (Max M), which can be used for medical expenses or purchasing Medicare program B, C or D. When a qualified retired person has a non-working spouse, both of the qualified retired person and spouse are covered by the Program A and share the 30%*TME /PA*C. When one qualified retired person passes away, the non-working spouse can carry left benefit balance. If there is more than one marriage involved, the left balance from the 30%*TME/PA*C is shared according to marriage yearly length.

Part #3:

The left portion such as SUM (20%*TME/PA*C) and extra over Max M are used for the government to pay for related Medicare expenses. Adjusting Max M affects Medicare balance. When Max M is decreased, there will be more Medicare taxes for the government. We need to set or adjust a reasonable Max M, which is similar to social security balance of earnings, expenses, and payments.

John H. Lee

4. PERSONAL LIFE BALANCE

When more people have balances physically, economically, and psychologically, problems and diseases will be reduced and more peace be achieved to improve individual life significantly.

Income balance

One of basic balances is about money. Income and expense are two major factors. Income should be more than expense at short and long terms. For individuals and families, balances between incomes, expenses, taxes, savings, and donations are very important. Mortgage payment of not more than 25-30% and savings at 10-25% of incomes are often suggested by financial advisors. The savings can be used for emergency, retirement, and next recession. Donations may be used to help relatives, friends, and non-profit organizations, who have real needs. Income and tax are quite constant for many people in many cases. Expense is the most changeable factor, which is needed to be adjusted, managed, and balanced according to actual incomes and situations. Making more or less income is not a problem. How to spend is significantly important. For company executives to balance investment, production, cost, sale, profit, share, and tax are also extremely important. When a recession comes, companies need to have at least a basic operation to maintain business and employment. Besides companies are for profit purpose, companies also have certain social responsibility. In the same way, governments do need to balance taxes, expenses, and emergency funds. It is the best to build self-supporting systems for different areas. When a recession comes, individuals, families, and governments can use emergency funds or savings to pay necessary expenses to avoid related problems.

A recession affects almost all people whether poor or rich. But some people (both poor and rich) are not affected significantly by a recession. When we check these people we find they have the common points: they have saved certain emergency funds, assets and savings and balanced their incomes and expenses well over time.

Jennifer and Bill had annual income of about sixty thousand dollars per year and own their house, which had a value of about one hundred seventy thousand dollars. They had two children at ages 6 and 9. They paid their mortgage payment at about eleven hundred per month. They purchased their house at one hundred thirty thousand dollars ten years ago. When they purchased their house, they paid the down payment of more than 20% and necessary closing fees to avoid a mortgage insurance and high interest rate. Before purchasing their house, they rented a one-bedroom apartment until they saved enough down payment to buy their house. Their food and clothing costs were about six hundred per month. One car loan cost them about three hundred per month for five years, at which time the interest rate was only 0.9 %. Another car was purchased with part of their savings and paid for with a one-time payment of five thousand dollars. They also paid insurances, house repairs, utilities, and other costs. They saved their 10% of income for IRA retirement. They had about ten thousand dollars as their emergency fund. They made their budget to save five thousand dollars or more per year. Besides eating outside few times per month, they liked to cut unnecessary costs as much as possible. They had their family vacation trip once almost every two years. When they had extra savings, they paid more for their mortgage and almost paid their mortgage off. During this recession, they purchased another house with more space for their family. Housing price was easily negotiated during this recession. They planned to keep and rent their old house to another family.

Jennifer and Bill's conditions are similar to many other mid-income families. They do budget each month, list all necessary and optional items, balance their income and expenses and have savings. Looks this recession does not affect their family. This recession helped them to buy a high-value house at a relatively low price.

MONTHLY INCOME BALANCE SHEET

Name(s) _____   Budget Date _____

Incomes: Source _____   Amount _____
           Source _____   Amount _____
           Source _____   Amount _____
                                 Total _____
Expenses: Item _____ Amount _____
           Item _____ Amount _____
           Item _____ Amount _____
           Item _____ Amount _____
           Item _____ Amount _____
           Item _____ Amount _____
           Item _____ Amount _____
                                 Total _____
Saving(S): _____
Retirement/IRA(R): _____
Donation(D):_____
Others: _____

Balance: Incomes = or > Expenses + S + R + D + Others .....(6)

Physical balance

Another basic balance is physical balance. Food intakes shall be balanced by metabolism, physical activities, and storage in the body. When storage in the body becomes more and more, nutritional balance is broken and overweight becomes a significant problem, which affects the immune system and causes many diseases such as high blood pressure, diabetes, eating more, expanded stomach, and lack of physical activities. Exercise, job, walk, house work, and many others relate to physical activities. Laziness may cause less productivity and affect brain function, which also effects the human body physically and psychologically. Unbalanced situations often cause these problems or even worse if actions to correct the imbalances are not taken.

In most developing countries, many people still have not enough food to eat to maintain their basic life. Starvation is a problem in many developing countries. Overweight is a serious problem currently in the United States. To keep healthy weight ranges from a medical point is suggested, which can be done when people balance their amount of food and physical activities. When sickness is involved, enough rest and proper methods are needed to recover. Self management plays an important role in keeping physical balance.

Psychological balance

When people worry more such as about their jobs, unemployment, emotional, relationship or others, serious pressure may cause depression, which may cause psychological unbalance. Psychological and physical balances are two important factors, which also relate to each other. Serious depression needs to be treated medically, which affects life quality and balances. Many people feel pressure in daily life even though our living conditions are much improved compared with situations 20 or 30 years ago. Some people have serious depression. Alcohol and drugs also cause many physical and psychological problems. Some people commit suicide to end their life. Having psychological balance can reduce depression and related problems, and help people to keep good mental health. How to handle different pressures can be solved by keeping balances without overpressure. Self management and professional help are needed to have psychological balance. Try to do our best, then to be happy.

Retired people, especially when they are sick, also need emotional care without serious loneliness from their children, friends, and society. Young adults need to balance different areas in their life for themselves, children, and parents. More and more retired people still have good health and like to contribute to their children and society, which could become good resources for families and society. Emotional and financial support between parents and children is very important.

Spiritual balance (See Chapter 8)

Time balance

Everybody has 24 hours per day. Some people have busy schedules and some not. Time needs to be balanced and distributed to do different things. There are various activities such as study, work, rest, talk, exercise, eating, sleeping, meeting, relaxing, cooking, and many others. We need to develop our potential according to our own physical, psychological, economic, and spirit abilities and capacities. If you are too busy, you need to list what are necessary and optional things to do. After finishing your necessary things, then you do optional things. When we have various focuses at different situations, we need to balance our time and life for basic peace at first. Then to achieve successfulness, happiness, joy, and love if possible.

Marriage

For adults, marriage and divorce are significant issues. In the United States, the divorce rate is about 50 % [20]. Some states require couples to have a period of waiting time such as one year for marriage consulting and more consideration before filing for divorce. Arguments and third-person involvements between married couples are two major reasons to cause divorces. How to manage money is a significant topic to cause arguments. Two major factors to a healthy marriage are commitment and patience. Marriage needs a long-term commitment. Doing almost anything needs commitment such as choosing a job, quitting smoking, changing bad habits or supporting family. Patience is one of the good personal characteristics. Couples need to balance between giving/receiving, love/loved and patience/argument, time distribution, and communication. Attitude and skill are two important factors. When arguments come, one or both of the couples need extra patience. Position exchange with your spouse may be considered for different situations. Balanced marriages have positive relationships with economic and emotional stabilities. When serious arguments happen, one of effective methods to overcome arguments is to pray or meditate for few minutes. More patient, wise, self controlled, and emotional management are needed to resolve related issues or problems. If the time is not enough, please take more time to pray, meditate or another method and come together without anger. Then related arguments may be overcome easily with patience, self control, wisdom, care, and love.

When married couples with children consider divorce, they need to think about the facts. Children feel safer and loved in a normal family with both father and mother. Children living with father and mother together usually do better in school, stay out of trouble, and follow the law. Also when they grow up, they keep better connections with parents, brothers and sisters and like to take care of elderly parents later. If possible, stay married for your children and yourselves.

Relationship

Almost everybody has different relationships and functions as multi positions as son or daughter, husband or wife, father or mother, brother or sister, cousin, friend, coworker, ABC member, and many others at the same time. A person needs to balance these different relationships and functions. Positive attitudes help to build good relationships. Of course different issues, problems, and arguments challenge relationships.

When serious relationship issues, problems or arguments are raised, we need to be rational and logical. To pray or meditate for few minutes may help us to have more patience, stable emotion, and wisdom for overcoming arguments. Prayer for more patience, wisdom, and self control is good to resolve issues or problems. The key is to have peace at first.

A balanced individual has many things in balance, such as income balance, emotional balance, time balance for different activities, physical balance, nutritional balance, relationship balance, and spiritual balance. The person is the center of these different balances. If somebody manages these balances well with good self management, he or she will have more peace and joy. It is the best to have right "Who, What, When, Where and Why" (5 W) as possible.

John H. Lee

5. POLITICAL PARTY AND GOVERNMENT POLICY

Political party and leader

Many potential government officers often promise or think many benefits including better life, right, pay, medical coverage, and social security to voters/people, which often are not practical and lack of long vision, during their campaigns or preparations to offices and shortly afterwards. After they have their power, they often consider their own purposes and benefits more important than their prior promises. When national budgets or deficits increase or even exceed maximums, then they have to cut expenses significantly and face reality or bankruptcy, which are then complained about by their voters/people. Finally, officers and voters/people begin to face their actual situations seriously and attempt to build fair policies for their realities at short and long terms.

Why do so many people like to become leaders even they need to pay a high price? The price is such as losing personal privacy, freedom, and normal life. Leaders are often criticized by many people and even receive threats by some extreme opponents sometimes. There are several major purposes for many people to like to become leaders: (1) to have more benefits; (2) to have more power; (3) to serve people; (4) to be more famous, and (5) combination of above purposes. We need to support leaders' service to people and good purposes and to limit their power and control their bad behaviors. For their benefits, transparent inspections, and financial records are needed publically to avoid corruptions. Of course benefits and power are two major issues. So we need to give leaders limited power, position length, benefits, and job range with clear descriptions. Also for major positions such as presidents, chairpersons, and governors, their terms need to be limited such as each leader can be the same position with maximum two terms in a life time. We need to make sure there is social stability after changing leaders.

Election by people or their representatives is a common form of democratic system. Election is a good form. The most important is for leaders to serve people. Elections are also often used by some politicians to divide people to cause more arguments or flights for their own political purposes, which causes more troubles to societies. In many countries, politicians often use power for their purposes. Election at high cost is an issue. Potential leaders often spend half of their time for collecting donations and use million and million dollars to support their campaigns and fight with others. Significant donations may create potential government corruptions in the future after these leaders are elected. There are some restricting regulations about political donations. If it costs too much to people and their countries, election contributions from individuals, companies, and organizations need to be limited to avoid negative effects. It is important to give potential leaders enough opportunities to express their views and plans how to run the country or state and follow people's congress if they are elected. If election by all people is too expensive, it may be better to elect their leaders by people's representatives. Also two-way directions are important from people to leaders and from leaders for people, which really means from people, by people and for people. To work together in the two ways is very important. Election is often easy from people to leaders. From leaders for people, which means for leaders to serve people and provide fair policies and solutions to many issues and problems for their countries and people, is even more important. In many countries, there are serious problems for leaders to serve people. Only the two-way directions between people and leaders can resolve serious social problems. From people, by people, and for people are needed to be together.

When people talk about the term "politicians", it has become a dirty word because many politicians often disappoint people for lack of their willingness to serve for people. Many politicians in many countries like to control power and consider their own benefits first and leave their people and countries behind. Transparency and inspection systems with fair policies can reduce or stop politicians and government officers to abuse power and obtain political purposes. This is one major reason why all dictators hate to build democratic and transparent systems in their countries. So their countries lack chances for long-term peaceful development.

Political parties have different ideas, philosophies, situations, attitudes, reviews, and positions. We need to avoid making unfair temporary government policies without long-term balances and considerations. Either "left" or "right" wings cannot provide long-term solutions. For example when the Democratic Party controls the Congress, they make and pass their preferred policies and laws. Later when the Republic Party has the control, they override these policies and laws. Such activities without both short and long-term considerations may lack balance and waste our social resources. When governments or government leaders promise public workers benefits such as pension plan, governments need to make sure these benefits are reasonable and practical and there really are enough funds to be set aside for these benefits. Otherwise future generations have to pay more prices for prior generations.

Incomes and benefits of elected or selected government leaders or officers should be stable and competitive but not higher compared with private industries to make sure they serve people and not for incomes, benefits, and power during their terms. Also after their terms such as at least for ten years, former elected or selected government leaders or officers shall not become political lobbyists to influence future government policies and laws.

Political party chairpersons often like to become government leaders, especially such as presidents, chairpersons, governors, and mayors. These public leaders should make their efforts and commitment and spend their working time for public work and serve their people and countries. Before taking their public officer positions, they should resign their leaderships as top positions for political parties. They serve public interests instead of prior political parties with special interests. Also they need to publish their personal properties and assets accurately before, during, and within such as ten years after their public services to avoid government corruption and abusing power for their own benefits. Compensations, benefits, and pensions to public officers shall be considered and set publically and carefully to make sure these public officers concentrate on their jobs and do not worry about their reasonable living standards. Their records are needed to be public and examined to avoid them to place their people and countries behind their own benefits. Also their power is needed to be balanced and examined to prevent and avoid overpower and corruption. Avoiding corruption from government officers is a very important matter.

Government policy and balance

There are two significant problems in many countries. One is that governments need more and more taxes to operate. Another is that individuals and businesses feel their tax rates of taxable incomes, sales, and properties are beyond their affordable ranges. They mean that increasing government operation efficiency is more beneficial than increasing tax rates. If a greater percentage of the taxes are used for non-necessary government workers, properties, and operations, then less of collected taxes are used for related projects, workers, people, and purposes. Governments should use limited resources for related services with short/long-term fair policies and plans.

The liberals like to have more taxes, large government, more benefits for poor and low-income people, which also means the government has more power and more support from low-income and poor people. The conservatives like to have smaller government, more personal responsibilities, and lower taxes, which also means government has less power over people's freedom and more income is kept by rich and mid-class people. The both sides need to be balanced for peaceful development. Our country needs both the liberals and the conservatives to consider balanced solutions, which are good for our short- and long-term development. People have freedom to express their ideas peacefully and not cause violence. They are responsible to follow the law. Our presidential voting rates are often 45-55%. If we consider Democrats and Republicans as the two legs to support and move the body (country), the left and right legs need to be balanced and adjusted to have strong support and balanced movement. When either the left or right leg moves too fast or too slow and the another leg cannot follow or against, then the body will lose its balance and fall down. It is very important for both the "Left' and "Right" to be balanced.

Governments need to tax rich people at reasonable high tax rates and help poor people with real needs, which may not become political issues when we find long-term balanced solutions. The liberals and the conservatives need to work together instead of fighting each other politically, which could use social resources efficiently and would reduce social costs. Politicians need to think how to provide fair policies and equal opportunities, improve social environments for reducing the number of poor people, and develop personal responsibilities and potentials for our country to be stable and have peaceful development.

We need to consider what we can do and what we need to do at the same time, which is a practical way. Additionally, it is important to tell the truth to people. Only after people know necessary and real information such as their social security balances, tax distributions, benefits, and government policies, then people can adjust their situations, plans, and actions to avoid future mistakes. People have a right to know and say the truth for making right decisions.

The health care bill was signed into a law in 2010, which may become a serious problem in the future. The bill divided Americans especially between Democrats and Republicans. If we have no enough money to support the bill for long term, then final progress will not be practical and not work. Even it looks like we have a "good" health care policy, the bill still does not work if we have more national budget shortage, deficit, and not enough personal responsibilities. In some countries, governments claim they have good health care policies for everybody. But normal and expensive medical operations need people to apply and wait for several years because lack of enough funds, which causes more people to delay or to die because doctors cannot treat patients on time. It also may cause more government corruptions, leading patients or their relatives to give government officers bribes (cash in most cases) to move related patient names on a waiting list from the bottom to the top for less waiting time. Then more and more people will complain and the system fails.

Democrats passed the health care bill in 2010. When conserve Republicans control Congress and Senate next time, I think that the bill will be debated again and may be removed in the near future, which will cause more social problems and damage our social resources. We must consider long-term practice and balance Democrats, Republicans, Independents, and others to make practical short- and long-term policies together, which may be modified in the future rather than totally change or remove. Before representatives of one group of people or political party present any bill or proposal, they need to think of other political parties or people. Then we can balance different people and reach permanent legal bills with short- and long-term purposes together. We need to avoid political ways to support some special people without fair balances and personal responsibilities, which waste our partial social resources and cause conflicts and class warfare.

To control carbon dioxide has become a national and international issue for reducing global warming, which also affects job creation. Coal, natural gas, and gasoline processes produce large amount of carbon dioxide. Also nuclear energy is not considered a very safe energy source after the exposure of the nuclear energy plant in Japan in 2011. Coal, natural gas, and gasoline are needed for people and many industries. Our government policy should have a balance between job creation and pollution control. Petroleum process and drilling in the United States not only creates more jobs but also stabilizes petroleum prices in international market, which relates to our national interests. Carbon dioxide needs to be reduced gradually and balanced with planting more trees and plants, which consume carbon dioxide and convert it into oxygen for people and animals. Some trees and plants can be used to produce food and bio fuel products. Other methods to utilize or store carbon dioxide can be also used. In firing-coal power plants, sulfide is a pollutant, which can be removed and converted into calcium sulfate, which can be used as a chemical or as a major ingredient for manufacturing drywall sheets. After finding good solutions to treat different industries, then we can create more jobs and keep clean air, land, and water. When the EPA has reasonable regulations to enforce, pollution issues and more jobs may be balanced at the same time.

It is better for us to build practical and fair policies from the beginning, which could be modified or adjusted further for long terms. Governments need to make fair policies with good benefits and to balance different people, industries, and environments.

Good governance

For both short and long-term visions, people like our governments to have good performance as good governance, which includes such as the follows:

(1) to have efficient operation to protect people and national interests at reasonable costs;

(2) to ensure food and life quality for people;

(3) to have mutual administration functions instead of political purposes;

(4) to prevent and punish corruptions;

(5) to be transparent with efficient inspection;

(6) to have fair short and long-term policies to cover and balance different factors;

(7) to balance government size (whether large or small) for meeting people's necessary needs with spending minimum tax as possible;

(8) to have democratic systems with real two-way contents from people to leaders and from leaders to serve people at low social costs as possible;

(9) to teach people to respect laws, democracy, freedom, human rights, responsibilities, balance, and peace;

(10) to have strong and effective security and military systems to protect peace and social order;

(11) to have fair foreign policies to balance national and foreign interests and to reach peace and

(12) to achieve a balanced, stable, rich, and peaceful country internally and externally.

6. TAX SIMPLIFICATION WITH FAIR RATES

Tax saving and fair rates

The government collects taxes from businesses and individuals. Both of fair tax rates and simplifying tax filing for reducing processing time and cost are important. Then more taxes can be used for more related projects and people. The IRS audited only about 1% of all individual tax returns filed in 2010 [21]. With some tax simplification, the IRS workers may spend more time to audit more tax filings and investigating potential crimes to avoid serious damages to our society such as Bernard Madoff's case. Income records may link to related tax payers' information to avoid false tax return crimes.

In our current tax system, individual tax rates are from 10% to 35% and corporation tax rates are from 15% to 35% according to different taxable incomes. Current individual taxes are figured from the Tax Table and Tax Computation Worksheet (2011) [22]. When individuals have taxable incomes not over $100,000, their tax numbers are searched and found from the Tax Table (2011), which has 12 pages. These tax numbers have no simple relationship with each other. People need to spend time to search and fill. Also, there is not a tool to check if related taxes or tax rates are in the right range or not. The IRS needs to store these numbers from the Tax Table. When these numbers and data are not part of simple formulas and calculated automatically, it increases operating costs. The key is for the government to balance taxes and operating costs.

Also the Tax Tables (2010 and 2011) provide unfair tax rates to individuals with low taxable incomes (less than $100), in which tax rates are such as 20%, 16% or 11%. The tax rate at the taxable income of $10,000 is only 10%. There is no reason for low taxable incomes to pay higher tax rates, which are shown in Tables 11 and 24.

More and more people, corporations, and the government would like to reduce time involved in the tax process, including tax filing and processing time, and reduce related government operating cost by simplifying our current tax systems. It was reported that Herman Cain presented a 9-9-9 flat tax plan for individual income tax, national sale tax, and corporation tax. Most local sale tax rates are already 6-9%. The difference between the current tax rates, 15-35% for corporations or 10-35% for individuals, and 9% is significant. Rick Perry presented 20% flat tax plan. Flat tax plans look simple and are easy to be put into operation. A flat tax rate is very simple and efficient as a sale tax rate, for it does not consider different incomes. But individuals and corporations have different taxable incomes. It is extremely difficult to cover different situations with one or several flat tax rates. Some people prefer to have a flat tax rate for all people with different taxable incomes, which is simple but not reasonable. For example a single individual has a taxable income of $20,000 and another single individual has a taxable income of $200,000. The initial difference is 10 times. If they pay taxes at a flat tax rate, such as 15%, there are respectively left with $17,000 and $170,000. The difference is still 10 times. If $15,000 is used for basic living costs, the first individual will have $2,000 left and the second will have $155,000 left after deducting the $15,000. The difference of the remaining amounts is 77.5 times (155000/2000). When they pay their taxes at 12.85% (=0.1+20,000/701,643) or 25.17% (=0.1804+200,000/2,804,367) respectively at the individual tax rates in 2011, their remaining amounts are $17,430 and $149,660 respectively. Their difference becomes 8.6 times, which is less than 10. After deducting $15,000, their remaining amounts are $2,430 and $134,660 respectively. The difference becomes 55.4 times (134660/2430), which is less than 77.5. Individuals and corporations should correspond to different tax rates reasonably according to their taxable incomes. Another area is for the government and lawmakers to provide fair and simple deductions, exemptions, capital gains, tax rates, and credits with less special interests as possible as good tax policy.

We all would agree that if we reduce our tax filing and processing time and costs by simplifying our current tax systems for individuals, businesses, federal and state governments, then more saved costs can be used for more related projects, programs, and people. Also we need to provide both fair and simple tax rates in order to save time and money. Individuals and businesses with high taxable incomes should pay higher tax rates. Here a liner/gradual (LG) tax system, a simple tax system, has been developed for different individuals and businesses. Tax rates are changed linearly or gradually when taxable incomes change. The LG Tax System may have these advantages: (1) current taxable income and withholding Tax Tables (12 pages et al.) and tax rate schedules are not needed; (2) easy taxable income ranges and tax rates are designed and adjusted; (3) calculation results may be compatible with minor differences comparing current tax systems (0 to 1% in Tables 11 and 24 and 0 to 0.4% in Tables 25 and 26); (4) a self-check tool for related tax rates is provided to check tax rate calculations, which may avoid or reduce calculation mistakes; (5) processing time and operation costs can be reduced significantly; (6) all information (for either individuals or businesses or both together) may be built into a database; and (7) tax data, such as total taxable incomes, average tax rates, total tax or tax projections, may be calculated, analyzed, estimated, and compared.

The LG Tax System converts all filing statuses, taxable incomes, tax rate formulas, tax rate range checks, names, IDs, tax rates, and tax calculations together into one simplified tax table. Tax rate formulas are connected with filing statuses and taxable incomes or income ranges. A calculated tax rate is checked with its correct tax rate range. Tax rates and tax calculations may be done automatically or manually. Automatic calculations may be done with a calculator or computer software product. Manual calculations are easily done by paper. The current income and withholding Tax Tables for federal and state governments may be not needed, replaced by compatible or new tax rate formulas. The LG Tax System simplifies current government tax systems and reduces processing time and costs significantly for individuals, corporations, and governments.

Tax for 4 individual filing statuses

In the current tax systems (2010 and 2011) [22, 23] for married couples filing jointly or qualifying widow(er), there are two parts. One part is the 12-page Tax Table. The second part includes the four tax computations as the follows:

Table 9 Current tax systems (2010 and 2011) for Married filing jointly or Qualifying widow(er)

Taxable income (TI) Over Not over	2010 Tax	Taxable income (TI) Over Not over	2011 Tax
0 100,000	Tax Table (12)	0 100,000	Tax Table (12)
100,000 137,300	0.25xTI-7,637.5	100,000 139,350	0.25xTI-7,750
137,300 209,250	0.28xTI-11,756.5	139,350 212,300	0.28xTI-11,930.5
209,250 373,650	0.33xTI - 22,219	212,300 379,150	0.33xTI-22,545.5
373,650	0.35xTI - 29,692	379,150	0.35xTI-30,128.5

Many individuals have taxable incomes less than $100,000 and need to search their tax from the 12-page Tax Table, which is long and takes time. There is no tax difference within one taxable income range such as $50,650-$50,700. There is no self-check tool for tax rates, which may cause related tax rate and tax calculation mistakes. Taxes in Tax Tables, tax computations, and income tax ranges in 2010 and 2011 have slight differences [22, 23], which are complex. All systems changes yearly and increase cost and time. To modify tax rates is much easy than to change all Tax Tables and taxable income ranges. If there is a simple tax system to combine Tax Tables, tax rate schedules and computations together practically, then current tax systems will be simplified significantly.

When people make more incomes, their taxable incomes shall be at reasonable high tax rates. Linear or gradual (LG) tax rate formulas are used for different taxable incomes. Tax rates change linearly or gradually when taxable incomes change, which relate to two typical simple math formulas of $y=a+bx$ and $y=c-d/x$. The tax rate (y) changes against taxable income (x) linearly or gradually, which are simple and practical. For $y=a+bx$, the slope is a constant b, which is neglected in the existing tax systems. For $y=c-d/x$, which is used by the IRS currently, the slope of y (tax rate) to x (TI) is not a constant (d/x^2). For married filing jointly with a taxable income not over $100,000, tax rates can be built on a linear increase basis:

Tax rate $= 0.1+TI/1,380,453$ (tax rate range check: 0.1- 0.173) ...(7)

Here $1/1,380,453$ (b) is a constant, which is the slope for $y=a+bx$ from $1/100,000/(0.17244-0.1)=1/1,380,453$. Tax rates change linearly by timing taxable income (from 0 to $100,000). The bottom tax rate is 0.1 or 10% (a).

Table 10 shows all LG tax rate formulas to different taxable incomes for married filing jointly or qualifying widow(er).

These formulas match 2011 Tax Table and computations. The taxable income ranges are designed into the easy four formats.

The tax rate range check is provided as a tool for self check, which means these calculated LG tax rates must be within their narrow range such as 0.1-0.173. These tax rate range checks can be used to avoid or reduce calculation mistakes.

Table 10 LG Tax System for Married jointly or Qualifying widow(er)

Filing Status	Taxable income (TI) Over	Not over	Tax rate formula	(range check)
(1/1)	0	100,000	$0.1+TI/1,380,453$	(0.1-0.173)
(1/2)	100,000	250,000	$0.1275+TI/2,226,312$	(0.172-0.240)
(1/3)	250,000	380,000	$0.1805+TI/4,213,608$	(0.239-0.271)
(1/4)	380,000		$0.35 - 30,128.5/TI$	(0.27-0.35)

Example: When a married couple has a taxable income $39,960, the tax rate formula is (1/1) $0.1+TI/1380453$ with the range check (10%-17.3%). Then $0.1+39960/1380453=12.89\%$ is its tax rate, which is within the range. The tax is $5,152.72. Tax rate and tax calculations can be done automatically or manually. The tax from $39,950 to $40,000 in the 2011 Tax Table is $5,146 at 12.88%. The $50 (40,000-39,950) causes 0.13% (50/39975). Their tax rate difference from the LG formula and 2011 Tax Table is only 0.01% (12.89%-12.88%).

The differences between the 2011 Tax Table (Married filing jointly or Qualifying widow(er)) and the LG formula (1/1) are compared in Table 11 and very compatible (0-1% differences). In the Tax Table (2011), the tax rates from 19.6%, 15.9%, 12.0% to 10.1% (*) for the low taxable income ranges from $5 to $1000 are unreasonable because the tax rates are from 10.0% to 17.2% for the taxable incomes from $10,000 to $100,000, which are shown in Table 11. These tax rates for the taxable income not over $100,000 should increase gradually from 10% to 17.2%. The tax rates calculated from the formula (1/1) are from 10.0% to 17.2% linearly, which are reasonable and practical. Processing time and cost will be reduced.

Table 11 Comparison of tax rates of 2011 Tax Table and LG Formula (1/1) for Married filing jointly or Qualifying widow(er)

Taxable Income ($)	2011 Tax Table Tax ($)	Tax rate	From Formula(1/1) (0.1+TI/1,380,453)	|Difference|
5.1	1	19.6% *	10.0%	9.6%
25.1	4	15.9% *	10.0%	5.9%
50.1	6	12.0% *	10.0%	2.0%
100.1	11	11.0% *	10.0%	1.0%
1,000	101	10.1% *	10.1%	0.0%
10,000	1003	10.0% *	10.7 %	0.7%
20,000	2154	10.8%	11.4%	0.6%
30,000	3654	12.2%	12.2%	0.0%
40,000	5154	12.9%	12.9%	0.0%
50,000	6654	13.3%	13.6%	0.3%
60,000	8154	13.6%	14.3%	0.7%
70,000	9756	13.9%	15.0%	1.1%
80,000	12256	15.3%	15.8%	0.5%
90,000	14756	16.4%	16.5%	0.1%
100,000	17244	17.2%	17.2%	0.0%

Table 12 shows the current tax systems for Head of household with the 12-page Tax Tables and tax computations. There is no self check for tax rate range. Tables 13 and 14

Table 12 Current tax systems for Head of household

Taxable income (TI) Over	Not over	2010 Tax	Taxable income (TI) Over	Not over	2011 Tax
0	100,000	Tax Table (12)	0	100,000	Tax Table (12)
100,000	117,650	0.25xTI-5,152.5	100,000	119,400	0.25xTI-5,232.5
117,650	190,550	0.28xTI-8,682	119,400	193,350	0.28xTI-8,814.5
190,550	373,650	0.33xTI-18,209.5	193,350	379,150	0.33xTI-18,482
373,650		0.35xTI-25,682.5	379,150		0.35xTI-26,065

show the current tax systems for Single and Married filing separately. Taxes in the Tax Tables, tax computations and taxable income ranges in 2010 and 2011 have slight differences.

Table 13 Current tax systems for Single

Taxable income (TI)		2010 Tax	Taxable income (TI)		2011 Tax
Over	Not over		Over	Not over	
0	100,000	Tax Table (12)	0	100,000	Tax Table (12)
100,000	171,850	0.28xTI-6,290.75	100,000	174,400	0.28xTI-6,383
171,850	373,650	0.33xTI-14,883.25	174,400	379,150	0.33xTI-15,103
373,650		0.35xTI-22,356.25	379,150		0.35xTI-22,686

Table 14 Current tax systems for Married filing separately

Taxable income (TI)		2010 Tax	Taxable income (TI)		2011 Tax
Over	Not over		Over	Not over	
0	100,000	Tax Table (12)	0	100,000	Tax Table (12)
100,000	104,625	0.28xTI-5,878.25	100,000	106,150	0.28xTI-5,965.25
104,625	186,825	0.33xTI-11109.5	106,150	189,575	0.33xTI-11272.75
186,825		0.35xTI-14,846	189,575		0.35xTI-15,064.25

LG Tax System for individuals and businesses

1. Federal tax simplification for individuals by LG Tax System

All Tax Tables (12 pages), tax calculation computations and schedules in the existing tax system for individuals are replaced by Table 15. Their taxable income ranges have been redesigned into convenient ranges. Tax rate formulas and range checks are connected with taxable income ranges, which simplify the current individual tax system and cover all calculations for all taxable incomes. Tax rate and tax calculations are done automatically or manually. The tax simplification will reduce tax processing time and cost. Total gross income record (I/R) is from employer(s) and other sources. When individuals (or businesses) file tax returns, their information link to their I/R, name, ID, and address, tax, and difference in Table 15 to avoid false tax return crimes. Database may be built from many individuals. Tax data such as tax rates, total taxable income, average tax rate, and total tax may be calculated, analyzed, projected, and compared.

Table 15 LG Tax System for federal individuals

Filing Status: (1)Married filing joint (2)Head of household (3)Single or (4)Married filing separately
Taxable income (TI):   I/R: Tax rate formula:
Range check: Tax rate: Tax:
Name: ID#:   Address:

All individual tax rate formulas for Filing Status (1), (2), (3) or (4): (The formulas match 2011 Tax Table and computations)

Filing Status	Taxable income (TI) Over	Not over	Tax rate formula	(range check)
(1/1)	0	100,000	0.1+TI/1,380,453	(0.1-0.173)
(1/2)	100,000	250,000	0.1275+TI/2,226,312	(0.172-0.240)
(1/3)	250,000	380,000	0.1805+TI/4,213,608	(0.239-0.271)
(1/4)	380,000		0.35 - 30,128.5/TI	(0.27-0.35)
(2/1)	0	100,000	0.1+TI/1,024,485	(0.1-0.198)
(2/2)	100,000	250,000	0.1586+TI/2,565,769	(0.197-0.257)
(2/3)	250,000	380,000	0.2074+TI/5,140,136	(0.256-0.282)
(2/4)	380,000		0.35 - 26,065/TI	(0.281-0.35)
(3/1)	0	60,000	0.1+TI/701,643	(0.1-0.186)
(3/2)	60,000	100,000	0.1396+TI/1,307,770	(0.185-0.217)
(3/3)	100,000	250,000	0.1804+TI/2,804,367	(0.216-0.270)
(3/4)	250,000	380,000	0.2298+TI/6,276,555	(0.269-0.291)
(3/5)	380,000		0.35 - 22,686/TI	(0.29-0.35)
(4/1)	0	70,000	0.1+TI/737,730	(0.1-0.195)
(4/2)	70,000	100,000	0.1357+TI/1,183,236	(0.194-0.221)
(4/3)	100,000	150,000	0.1511+TI/1,446,480	(0.22-0.255)
(4/4)	150,000	200,000	0.1953+TI/2,521,008	(0.254-0.275)
(4/5)	200,000		0.35 - 15,064/TI	(0.274-0.35)

When a taxable income $90,048 is inputted for a single individual, the tax rate formula of (3/2) 0.1396+TI/1,307,770 is connected. The range check is (0.185-0.217). The tax rate is 0.1396+90,048/1,307,770=20.85% within the range. The tax is $18,775.01 (20.85%x90048). Tax rate and tax calculations can be done automatically or manually. The tax from the 2011 Tax Table is $18,824 at 20.90%. Their tax rate difference is only 0.05% (20.90%-20.85%). More or all individual income data may be built into their database for analysis.

The tax rates between the 2011 or 2010 Tax Tables, tax computations and schedules for different filing statuses and the LG tax rate formulas are very compatible in most cases. Tables 11 and 24 show 0 to 1% differences. Tables 25 and 26 show 0 to 0.4% differences.

If during a recession, governments may promote more purchases and job creation by reducing tax rates such as from 10-35% to 5-30% for individuals or 15-35% to 5-25% for businesses by a simple subtraction in the tax rate formulas with 5% (or 10%). For example for married filing jointly with taxable incomes from $250,000 to $380,000, the formula may be converted into 0.1305+TI/4,213,608 (0.189-0.221) or for corporations with taxable incomes not over $100,000 into 0.05+TI/1,379,310 (0.05-0.1225) easily.

2. Tax simplification for federal individual and business filings

All federal tax filings for both individuals and businesses in the United States may be converted into the Table 16, which may simplify and unite all federal tax systems and data together. Tax rate formulas are connected with related filing statuses and taxable incomes. The tax data, which are collected from Table 16, may be calculated, analyzed, and projected. Their database may be built. The tax simplification will reduce tax processing time and cost significantly.

Table 16 LG Tax System for federal individual and business filings

---

Filing Status 1: (1) Individual or (2) Business
Filing Status 2: (a)Married filing joint (b)Head of Household
(c)Single or (d)Married filing separately
Filing Status 3: (f)Cigarette Products (h)Corporation… (p)Retailers…
Taxable income (TI):   I/R: Tax rate formula:
Range check: Tax rate: Tax:
Name: ID#:   Address:

For (1) Federal individuals, tax rate and tax calculations are shown in Table 15. For (2/h) Federal business corporation tax, the tax rate formulas are shown in Table 17.

Table 17 LG Tax System for federal corporations
(The formulas simplify the Tax Computations in 2010 and 2011)

Filing Status	Taxable income (TI) Over	Not over	Tax rate formula	(range check)
(2/h/1)	0	50,000	0.15	
(2/h/2)	50,000	100,000	$0.0775+TI/689{,}655$	(0.15-0.223)
(2/h/3)	100,000	335,000	$0.39-16{,}750/TI$	(0.222-0.34)
(2/h/4)	335,000		$0.35 - 3{,}350/TI$	(0.34-0.35)

$$\text{Total Tax}=0.15*\text{SumTIm}+0.0775*\text{SumTIn}+\text{Sum}(TI*TI)n/689655$$
$$+0.39*\text{SumTIo}-16750*o+0.35*\text{SumTIp}-3350*p \ \ldots\ldots (8)$$

Here m, n, o, and p are business numbers during the four taxable income ranges. The total tax equation (8) or similar equations may be used to estimate future tax projections or analyze tax data.

3. Tax simplification for all federal and state tax filings (individuals and businesses)

All federal and state tax filings for both individuals and businesses in the United States may be converted into the Table

John H. Lee

18, which can simplify and unite all tax systems and data together. Tax rate formulas are connected with related filing statuses and taxable incomes. The tax data, which are collected from Table 18, may be calculated, analyzed, and projected. Their database can be built. The tax simplification will reduce tax processing time and cost significantly.

Table 18 LG Tax System for federal and state individuals and businesses

---

Fling Status 1: (1)Federal (2)Alabama … (17)Iowa … (51)Wyoming
Filing Status 2: (101) Individual or (102) Business
Filing Status 3: (a)Married filing joint (b)Head of Household
      (c)Single or (d)Married filing separately
Filing Status 4: (f)Cigarette Products (h)Corporation... (p)Retailers...
Taxable income (TI):   I/R: Tax rate formula:
Range check: Tax rate: Tax:
Name: ID#:   Address:

For (1/101) Federal individuals, tax rate and tax calculations are shown in Table 15. For (1/102) Federal business corporation tax, the tax rate formulas are shown in Table 17. Tables 19 and 21 show the LG tax rate formulas for Iowa individuals and corporations.

Table 19 Iowa individual LG formulas for all filing statuses (2011)

Filing Status	Taxable income(TI) Over Not over	Tax rate formula	(range check)
(17/101/1)	0 20,000	TI / 470,588	(0 - 0.0425)*
(17/101/2)	20,000 100,000	0.035+TI/2,661,698	(0.0425-0.07257)*
(17/101/3)	100,000	0.0898-1,723/TI	(0.07257-0.0898)

---

* The two LG Tax formulas simplify Iowa 2011 Tax Tables (5 pages), which is shown in Table 20.

Table 20 IA1040 Tax Tables 2011 for all filing statuses (5 pages)

Taxable income		Tax $	Taxable income		Tax $
Over	Not over		Over	Not over	
150	400	1	30,000	30,050	1,489
400	700	2	30,050	30,100	1,492
			....		
5,000	5,050	68	50,000	50,050	2,925
			....		
10,000	10,050	278	70,000	70,050	4,565
			....		
20,000	20,050	842	90,000	90,050	6,361
....			95,400	95,450	6,846

Table 21 Iowa corporation tax rate formulas and range check
(The formulas match the Tax Computations in 2011)

Filing Status	Taxable income (TI)		Tax rate formula	(range check)
	Over	Not over		
(17/102/h/1)	0	25,000	0.06	
(17/102/h/2)	25,000	100,000	0.08 - 500/TI	(0.06-0.075)
(17/102/h/3)	100,000	250,000	0.1 - 2,500/TI	(0.075-0.09)
(17/102/h/4)	250,000		0.12 - 7,500/TI	(0.09-0.12)

4. Federal tax simplification for individuals (2010) by LG Tax System

Table 22 shows the good match to all the 2010 Tax Table and computations of the IRS system for individuals (4 filing statuses) [23]. Their original taxable income ranges are kept. Tax rate formulas and range checks are connected with related taxable income ranges. Table 22 simplifies the individual tax system and covers all calculations for all taxable incomes under different filing statuses. Tax rate and tax calculations can be done automatically or manually. Tax data from its database may be calculated, analyzed, projected, estimated, and compared.

Table 22 LG Tax System for federal individuals (2010)

Filing Status:(1)Married filing joint (2)Head of Household (3)Single
  or (4)Married filing separately.
Taxable income (TI):   I/R: Tax rate formula:
Range check: Tax rate: Tax:
Name: ID#:   Address:

All individual tax rate formulas for Filing Status (1), (2), (3) or (4):
(The formulas match 2010 Tax Table and computations)

Filing Status	Taxable income (TI) Over	Not over	Tax rate formula	(range check)
(1/1)	0	100,000	0.1 + TI / 1,358,142	(0.1-0.174)
(1/2)	100,000	373,650	0.1382 + TI / 2,823,892	(0.173-0.271)
(1/3)	373,650		0.35 - 29,692 / TI	(0.27-0.35)
(2/1)	0	100,000	0.1 + TI / 1,015,486	(0.1-0.199)
(2/2)	100,000	373,650	0.1683 + TI/3,306,266	(0.198-0.282)
(2/3)	373,650		0.35 - 25,682 / TI	(0.281-0.35)
(3/1)	0	60,000	0.1 + TI / 693,642	(0.1-0.187)
(3/2)	60,000	100,000	0.1406 + TI/1,309,053	(0.186-0.218)
(3/3)	100,000	171,850	0.28 - 6,290 / TI	(0.217-0.244)
(3/4)	171,850	373,650	0.33 - 14,883 / TI	(0.243-0.291)
(3/5)	373,650		0.35 - 22,356 / TI	(0.29-0.35)
(4/1)	0	70,000	0.1 + TI / 728,191	(0.1-0.197)
(4/2)	70,000	100,000	0.1378+TI/1,198,972	(0.196-0.222)
(4/3)	100,000	104,625	0.28 - 5,878 / TI	(0.221-0.224)
(4/4)	104,625	186,825	0.33 - 11,109 / TI	(0.223-0.271)
(4/5)	186,825		0.35 - 14,846 / TI	(0.27-0.35)

When a married couple has a taxable income $39,960, the tax rate formula is (1/1) 0.1+TI/1358142 with the range check (10%-17.4%), which is connected with the taxable income under the filing status. The tax rate is 0.1+39960/1358142=12.94%, which is within the range. The tax is $5,170.82. Tax rate and tax calculations can be done automatically or manually. The tax from $39,950 to $40,000 in the 2010 Tax Table is $5,159 at 12.91%. Their tax rate difference is only 0.03% (12.94%-12.91%).

There are slight tax differences in the Tax Tables, tax computations and income tax ranges in 2010 and 2011, which are shown in above Tables 9, 12, 13 and 14. Their LG tax rate formulas are also slightly different, which are shown in Table 23.

Table 23 LG formula comparison for 2010 and 2011

Filing Status	Taxable income(TI) Over	Not over	Rate Formula(2010)	Rate Formula(2011)
(1/1)	0	100,000	0.1+TI/1,358,142	0.1+TI/1,380,453
(2/1)	0	100,000	0.1+TI/1,015,486	0.1+TI/1,024,485
(3/1)	0	60,000	0.1+TI/693,642	0.1+TI/701,643
(3/2)	60,000	100,000	0.1406+TI/1,309,053	0.1396+TI/1,307,770
(4/1)	0	70,000	0.1+TI / 728,191	0.1+TI/737,730
(4/2)	70,000	100,000	0.1378+TI/1,198,972	0.1356+TI/1,183,236

For married couples filing jointly, when their taxable income (TI) is $50,001, its tax rates are 0.1+50001/1358142=13.68% in 2010 and 0.1+50001/1380453 =13.62% in 2011. Their tax rate difference is only 0.06% (TI/1358142 – TI/1380453).

Besides designing taxable income ranges into easy format in Tables 10 and 15, tax rates can be designed and adjusted according to actual situations every year. For example a tax rate range is designed to 21.0% at taxable income $100,000 or 27.0% at $250,000 and their tax rates change linearly within the range, then their tax rate formula is 0.17+TI/2,500,000.

The tax rate differences between the 2011 or 2010 Tax Tables and tax computations for four different filing statuses and the LG tax rate formulas are very compatible in most cases. Besides Table 11, Table 24 shows the tax rate differences between the 2011 Tax Table and LG formula for Head of household with the taxable income range not over $100,000, which are compatible with 0-1% differences. Table 25 shows the tax rate differences between the 2011 tax rates from the current tax computations with the complex taxable income ranges and the LG formulas with the convenient taxable income ranges for "Head of household", which are compatible with 0-0.4%. Table 26 shows the tax rate differences for single individuals, which are compatible with 0-0.4%.

Table 24 Comparison of tax rates between 2011 Tax Table and LG Formula for Head of household (Taxable Income: not over $100,000)

Taxable Income ($)	2011 Tax Table Tax ($)	Tax rate	From LG Formula (0.1+TI/1,024,485)	|Difference|
5.1	1	19.6% *	10.0%	9.6%
25.1	4	15.9% *	10.0%	5.9%
50.1	6	12.0% *	10.0%	2.0%
100.1	11	11.0% *	10.0%	1.0%
1,000	101	10.1% *	10.1%	0.0%
10,000	1003	10.0% *	11.0 %	1.0%
20,000	2396	12.0%	12.0%	0.0%
30,000	3896	13.0%	12.9%	0.1%
40,000	5396	13.5%	13.9%	0.4%
50,000	7274	14.6%	14.9%	0.3%
60,000	9774	16.3%	15.9%	0.4%
70,000	12274	17.5%	16.8%	0.7%
80,000	14774	18.5%	17.8%	0.7%
90,000	17274	19.2%	18.8%	0.4%
100,000	19761	19.8%	19.8%	0.0%

Tax simplification shall be our first target to reach practically, which can reduce significant time and costs for individuals, businesses, and governments. Then the second target is fair tax rates, which shall be fair to both of the government and individuals/businesses. There is a balance between taxes and government operating costs, which takes time to figure out. Their database analysis and projection may help the process.

Table 25 Comparison of tax rates from Tables 12 and 15 (2011) for Head of household (Taxable Income: $100,000 - $1,000,000)

Taxable Income ($)	2011 tax rates (Tax/TI, Table 12)	LG Formulas (Table 15)	|Difference|
100,000	19.8%	19.8%	0.0%
120,000	20.7%	20.5%	0.2%
140,000	21.7%	21.3%	0.4%
160,000	22.5%	22.1%	0.4%
180,000	23.1%	23.0%	0.1%
200,000	23.8%	23.7%	0.1%
230,000	25.0%	24.8%	0.2%
250,000	25.6%	25.6%	0.0%
290,000	26.6%	26.4%	0.2%
320,000	27.2%	27.0%	0.2%
350,000	27.7%	27.6%	0.1%
380,000	28.1%	28.1%	0.0%
400,000	28.5%	28.5%	0.0%
1,000,000	32.4%	32.4%	0.0%

Different people have different ideas about their money and government taxes. Some people would like to pay lower taxes and give more in donations to charities. Some people would like to pay higher taxes to support the government. Some religious people would like to support their churches with donations. Some people would like to pay taxes only and keep the remaining money for themselves. Some people would like to support education for children with special needs. Some environmentally friendly people would like to support environment research projects with more funds. Some people would like to give more money to non-profit organizations. Some people would like to have money for their children. Some people would like to support scholarships for outstanding students. Some people would like to give their financial support to cancer research and patients. Government policies should cover different people and companies. Besides taxes to the government, which have to be paid, all donations to charities, churches, governments, and non-profit organizations may be optional for people who have that preference and should be tax deductable. Individuals or companies with different ideas may donate their extra money to charities, schools, or the government, which may reduce significant conflicts between the liberals and the conservatives.

Table 26 Comparison of tax rates from Tables 13 and 15 (2011) for Single (Taxable Income: $100,000 - $1,000,000)

Taxable Income ($)	2011 tax rates (Tax/TI, Table 13)	LG Formulas (Table 15)	|Difference|
100,000	21.6%	21.6%	0.0%
120,000	22.7%	22.3%	0.4%
140,000	23.4%	23.0%	0.4%
160,000	24.0%	23.7%	0.3%
180,000	24.6%	24.5%	0.1%
200,000	25.4%	25.2%	0.2%
230,000	26.4%	26.2%	0.2%
250,000	27.0%	27.0%	0.0%
290,000	27.8%	27.6%	0.2%
320,000	28.3%	28.1%	0.2%
350,000	28.7%	28.6%	0.1%
380,000	29.0%	29.0%	0.0%
400,000	29.3%	29.3%	0.0%
1,000,000	32.7%	32.7%	0.0%

Different tax rates, taxes, and total taxes may be calculated, adjusted, compared, and projected. The U.S. national debt of $15 trillion may be reduced over time, such as over 10, 20 or 50 years, which can be done with related equations similar to the social security balance in Chapter 2. The factor "G" includes prior balances and adjustments. These calculations, adjustments, and projections should be done professionally instead of politically. Total tax amount shall be more or equal to sum of government operating costs and emergency fund. There are many items and numbers involved, yet the concept of balance lies behind all of them. More budget and deficit data are available at www.whitehouse.gov/omb/budget.

7. POOR AND RICH PEOPLE
AND IMMIGRATION

Balance for poor and rich people

There are always poor and rich people in every country of the world. We need to avoid allowing government officers and the rich to control social resources, becoming even richer while the poor have little or no social resources, becoming even poorer, which usually cause serious social conflicts or even wars if there are significant imbalances between the rich and the poor. Also issues surrounding the poor should not be used for political, power, and other unfair gains. Otherwise more and more poor people are produced, leaving governments, churches, non-profit organizations, and societies to support a growing population of the poor. We need to reduce poverty problems.

According to the U.S. Census Bureau (September, 2010), overall poverty was at 15.7 percent, or 47.8 million people, which was an increased from the 2009 report at 14.3 percent, or 43.6 million people. It means 157 in 1000 Americans in 2010 were struggling in poverty for their food, living expenses, medical care, and other basic living costs.

People agree that rich people need to pay relatively more taxes at reasonably high tax rates to contribute to our society and help the poor and disabled on the basis of real needs. The government usually distributes social resources. Personal responsibilities are also very important. We need to have balance, paying attention to different negative situations, making sure not to produce more dependent adults and special groups of people. The "poor people" should not become a political issue. Overspending is a serious issue from individuals and governments. Proper distribution of social resources is very important. We need to avoid class warfare.

Social welfare such as food stamp and Medicaid should be offered to poor people with real needs after considering all personal incomes, assets, properties, savings, and any valuable objects. Poor people with real needs do need help from families, relatives, governments, and societies. People with no or low incomes do not mean they are poor people. Some people may have more cash, properties or assets from their savings, parents or other sources even they have no or low incomes. It was reported in March, 2012 that a lady, who won $1 million in the Michigan State Lottery and owned her two houses and one new car, still collected her food stamps from the government [24]. Another report was in December, 2011 that a woman in Washington State received the state economic benefits when she lived in a $1 million waterfront home on Lake Washington [25]. A person is qualified to apply for social welfare programs shall include all personal income, saving, property, and asset, which is similar to apply for additional social security payment.

Our society should provide people equal opportunities. People can reach their basic living standard (food, rent, utilities, clothes, and basic medical insurance) affordably through their normal jobs. Hard work and/or good training can help people reach even better living standards beyond the basic living standard, which should not be a problem.

Governments need to make fair and balanced policies to tax rich people at reasonably high tax rates, middle class people at reasonably mid tax rates and poor people at reasonably low tax rates based on their taxable incomes, which are discussed in Chapter 6. Additionally governments need to promote or provide equal opportunities, practical training, and related tools for poor people to become independent and develop their responsibilities and potentials. Governments also need to help the poor and disabled with real needs as possible. However these people need to take their own responsibilities as much as possible. All people working together can reduce or even further resolve poverty problems. Our society needs the rich to bear a greater responsibility to society.

For helping poor people, the best way is to provide necessary tools and opportunities to the poor. They need to improve and change their situations through their work. Only providing money lasts only for short period of time. For example there are homeless people, who are extremely poor, in almost every country. Governments, churches, non-profit organizations, relatives, and friends should provide temporary places and food for them plus their commitment to have change and training without drugs and alcohol. Then after proper training for a period of time, most of them could be ready to go into the labor force or market place for themselves to survive for their basic living needs. Another example is that there are some girls or women, who have children without marriage and get supports from governments. Even several children in a single family are from different fathers without support from these fathers, who shall be responsible. The governments need to ask these fathers to be responsible. Child supports are transferred from their employers directly. Our society and government do need to help these children with real needs. When basic living conditions differ between their working or living on government welfare is very close, then they usually prefer to not work. Also many couples in the United States adopt children from foreign countries every year.

Each adoption often costs $15,000 to $25,000. When some parents cannot be responsible for their children, adoption or foster family is one good option to let responsible adults to raise these children, which is good for the children.

Many factors are involved in whether a person is poor, middle class or rich. What individuals do in their lives and how they spend their incomes are important factors. Around environment is another important factor, which is not easy for individuals to change. If the environment factor is favorable to someone, he or she still has related problems if there is no enough work. There are many reasons to be poor such as overspending, low income, less work, serious sickness, high medical expense, failed business, lack of personal responsibility, less skill, less knowledge, lack of opportunities, and less experience. Personal responsibility is very important.

In many poor and closed countries, most people or even up to 80% of populations are poor with very low basic living standards. Unemployment rates are usually high or productivity is low. Government officers and rich people control most social resources. Most poor people usually wish to have their leaders to save them or give them a better life. Leaders with communism, "faithful" or theocracy minds are welcome by most poor people. When leaders have low to mid incomes and show people they care and are close to them, then poor people would trust their leaders and give away their rights to their leaders confidently. These leaders can do what they want to do after earning the trust from poor people. Of course these leaders often like to not tell people truth, and get more benefits for themselves without public information and inspection. These leaders usually let poor people to be brain washed without truth and fair knowledge and then poor people may live a life "faithful" to their leaders without freedom and individual potential development. When leaders have high incomes like the rich and do not show care and are not close to poor people, government corruptions often happen and almost all poor people will then hate their leaders and wish their new leaders to get power, which often happens through violence or wars. There are strong conflicts even wars between poor and rich people. Poor people usually complain that they lack opportunities and equal rights because rich people take their rights away.

In open countries, people usually can obtain real information publically and can have a good education and more opportunities. That people with good health are in poor situations is often considered because of their unemployment, sickness, overspending habit or lazy behavior. Government's fair policies and more opportunities play important roles in converting more poor people into middle class or rich people by developing individual potential and responsibility. Improvements take steps with gradual achievements over time, which needs stable social environments. It is very important to balance the poor and the rich, which affects societal stability and a country's peaceful development.

Poor people often have been called to gain equal rights and opportunities through class warfare by many leaders. During the past thousand years in many countries, our histories have shown that class warfare has caused significant violence and wars. Karl Marx (1818 – 1883) was a German political economist, revolutionary activist, and sociologist. He converted the poor and rich and poverty problems into the simple class problem and suggested the poor or workers to unite for class struggle and warfare with social revolution. He was a scholar, who often was in poor status, and designed a final idealistic society (communism) to provide distributions according to people's needs and to work according to their personal ability, which attracted many people, especially poor and young people, without deep considerations. Class struggle and warfare have caused social orders to be destroyed, people to die, and the environments to be damaged. For example the Liberation Warfare (from 1945 to 1949) in China, resulted more than three million people dead and millions and millions of people became refugees and lived in poverty [26-28].

A society is very complex. People's financial and social positions often change after certain periods of time. Class warfare is a simple or extreme method, which usually causes violence and wars for one class or group of people against other(s). Violence and warfare damage and destroy social order, laws and government function, kill people, and damage environments. Class warfare is often repeated and continued on a circular basis, which causes even more poverty and social problems, and affects people's life significantly in many countries. People have learnt from our histories that these social conflicts between poor and rich people can be balanced and resolved through non-violent or peaceful development. Proper tax rates, proper distribution, personal responsibilities, work opportunities, social resource sharing, social services, and other methods can be used to resolve social conflicts and problems among the poor, rich and middle class.

When people risk their ideas, investments, innovations, products, services, and hard work, only a portion of businesses survive or grow after certain years. Businesses create more jobs for people and social responsibility. Many new businesses are closed after five or ten years, which mean they lost their investments and time. These successful people need to have reasonable rewards and pay reasonably high tax rates. Taxes can be used to help the poor with real needs after they fulfill their own responsibilities. Not only the poor and rich issue, but also there are many other issues such as different background and faiths. To manage these differences in a balanced way for peaceful development is the best method to build a harmonious society with peace at low social cost.

Looks money is a significant issue in poor countries. Governments print more money which usually causes more inflation because there is no balance between products and money. But when printed money, which is used as investment or loan, is used in the cycle of investment or loan, employment, production, product, service, sale, and profit, then more employment reduces the number of poor people, allowing more people to be responsible and become middle-class people, reducing social conflicts between the poor and the rich. These borrowers (individuals or corporations) have a personal and social responsibilities to manage money with restricted regulations such as a limit to personal incomes of the borrowers until they pay their loans back to the governments. Then similar steps may be reproduced and continued. The governments may take certain amount of printed money away from the market to control inflation. In these cases, the printed money by the governments has positive effects.

Immigration and issue

Development situations are different from one area to another area or from one country to another country. People often like to migrate to developed areas in their country or immigrate to developed countries for more opportunities, equal rights, and a better quality of life. Immigration has more complex issues than migration.

Many countries have short- and long-term immigration needs. Some countries may have high unemployment and need investors. Almost every country issues the immigration visa to qualified investors. Some countries may have needs such as more laborers, military soldiers, nurses or scientists because of shortages of these kinds of people. So immigrants can do things such as agricultural work, military security, take care of old and sick people or develop science and technology for these countries. When some countries are rich and have more opportunities and fair policies, people from other countries like to go to these countries. Many developed countries have low birth rates, which mean stable populations cannot be kept or will decrease after 20-50 years. Immigration may also affect many issues such as job market, tax, social resource, education, medical service, law, culture, language, security, national conflict, faith, religion, and other areas. If these issues are not addressed properly, they would become serious problems and affect social stability.

Things such as different cultures, languages, and religions may give benefits to a country, especially in an immigration country like the United States. When people can speak different languages, their country connects with other countries more easily and have more social resources. Also if immigration issues are not handled with balances properly by people and governments, some of them will become serious problems especially when two or more problems are combined together if there are no official common grounds. For example, immigrants speak different languages. Most immigrants prefer to speak their own languages and teach their children to speak their own mother-country languages. If a large group of immigrants speak a special language, which is different from their country's official language, then a government allows their special language to become one of the official languages. Plus if these immigrants have another special religion, race or nationality and follow their own laws, they then possibly seek independence after certain years such as 100 years. During their process to be independent, there would be more social conflicts, violence or even war in that country.

For languages, there are good benefits that people can speak different languages to connect with other countries. But their officially national language should be one or less as possible. Even old immigrants may have difficulty in learning a new language, but their children have to learn their official language in schools. All children need to learn our national history and respect the U.S. laws. Religious and non-religious faiths often contribute peace and good moral standards to our community and the world. Also people with different religious and non-religious faiths often consider only their faiths are right and do not have peace with others, do not respect others, like to "force" others to believe their faiths or even often cause violence and even wars. Peace and secular laws should be our common grounds. Culture is another sensitive issue.

The economic issue is a basic factor. When our country needs more foreign workers, we like foreign workers to work for U.S. companies. When our country has a recession or more unemployment, we do not need more foreign workers and let them to leave. Many countries have similar situations. We need to make friendly and practical policies for our country and these foreign workers. Some of them may stay and become illegal immigrants. Most illegal immigrants come to or stay in the United States for economic reason. Most first-generation immigrants are usually hard-working. Some state governments give low-income immigrants public welfare. Many governments require legal immigrants to have personal financial support and not to take public welfare before issuing the immigrant visa. For social security benefits, there is the policy to require 10-years work for 40-credit eligibility and then to qualify.

Poor people and immigration issues relate to many areas. If we do not handle them properly, many problems have been and will be raised. Here are a few examples.

California has had "good" welfare programs compared with other states. It was reported that In FFY 2010, $41 billion was used to support programs that directly assisted millions of Californians [29], including:

• 3.9 million Californians who received food assistance through the Supplemental Nutrition Assistance Program (SNAP), known as CalFresh in California;
• 2.6 million California households who received federal Earned Income Tax Credit;

• Nearly 1.3 million low-income seniors and people with disabilities who received cash assistance through the Supplemental Security Income (SSI) Program; and

• More than 1 million jobless Californians who receive UI benefits.

Many poor people and immigrants have gone to California for related welfare programs for many years. It was reported that California had serious shortage in its budget in 2010. Unbalanced budget has become a serious problem in California, which is a significant challenge.

S.J. and D.A. immigrated to the United States from a foreign country through their daughter, who was an U.S. citizen and provided personal financial support. After they lived with their daughter's family for half year, they moved to California because the State of California offered more welfare programs and low-income benefits to poor citizens, residents, and immigrants. So they did not need to get their daughter's personal financial support. Then they lived in California, applied and received their welfare and low-income benefits from the state government. Even they owned their property, had retirement and savings in their home country, which were not written in their application documents.

Governments, non-profit organizations, churches, families, and friends do need to help the poor with real needs as possible. Also personal responsibility plays a very important role.

Illegal immigration

The United States has been a rich country with more opportunities, fair policies, and stable environments for many years. We are proud of such achievements. We need to give and require people including illegal immigrants to have both opportunities and responsibilities at the same time.

Almost every country likes to attract investors and intellectuals for more employment and future development as a long-term plan and use some foreign workers to provide a temporary work force for such as agricultural, energy, and construction industries as a short-term plan. We do need to make friendly policy to attract more legal immigrants, who can make good contributions to our society. We also need to balance our immigration policy for short and long terms.

Illegal immigration is a tough problem in the United States, which also relates to the U.S. national security. More illegal immigrants entering the United States provide a serious risk for terrorists to also pass our boarders, which affect our national security. It is estimated there may be 12 million illegal immigrants from foreign countries in the United States now. Some of them have no records. How then is it possible for us to ask these immigrants to be responsible for their illegal behavior when they break our laws? We need to make related policies and laws to reduce or avoid future illegal immigrants entering our boarders, and also to provide as strong a national security as possible. We need to face the problems and help these illegal immigrants in the United States to be in the open rather than in hiding to avoid or reduce management, crime, and terrorism problems. How to deal with these illegal immigrants, who are already in the United States, will affect future illegal immigration and our national security.

The following comments may be suggested for dealing with illegal immigration issues while encouraging opportunities and responsibilities at the same time.

1. Our boarders need to be protected seriously at first. Partial military forces may be removed from German and Japan to be used for protecting our own boarders to reduce its operational cost. Our military forces in Germany and Japan can be kept to minimum numbers. Military technologies such as long-distance rockets, robots, nuclear weapons, and computer

controllers have changed military methods. Moving military forces may take a few days in current situations by airplane transportation. They are totally different from the situations fifty years ago.

2. Increase fines and punishments if businesses or companies hire illegal immigrants without proper legal working documents;

3. Allow illegal immigrants, who have lived in the United States for more than certain years such as 5 years illegally, to apply for a special temporary working visa, which is different from normal working visa H1. They need to provide their no crime record certificates and passports or travel documents from their country governments or embassies. The special temporary working visa needs to be reissued every 3 years with a maximum renew such as 5 times. Illegal immigrants may have strong and physical connection with their home countries. Different working permit formats can be recognized and inspected easily. Within such as every 3 years, they need to go back to their home countries for at least one week. Employers need to provide employment documents for them;

4. If illegal immigrants have already married U.S. citizens, they can apply for another special visiting visa. The visa needs to be reissued at a predetermined interval, such as every 5 years;

5. All illegal adult immigrants, who live in the United States, have no right to apply for permanent residence and citizenship because they are breaking the U.S. immigration law and affect our national security. There may be a second chance by their responsible behavior. If they go back to their home countries and live there for a certain period of time (such as 5 years or more), then they can be eligible to apply for normal visa applications or for permanent residence if they are qualified through the U.S. embassies in their countries according to the U.S. immigration law.

6. Illegal immigrants need to pay social security, Medicare, and income tax as other people. After they go back and retire in their countries, the portion of their own contributions to social security and Medicare can be paid gradually to them through the U.S. embassies in their countries where they live according to the U.S. social security regulations. Then illegal immigrants may have additional payments during their retirement in their own countries. People in their countries may know more about the U.S. reality through those illegal immigrants rationally.

7. When illegal immigration children go to college, their student legal status may be as foreign students. They pay tuition fees at in state, out of state or foreign student rates depending on their parents' situations. After 18 years old, they may follow related regulations and apply for the above temporary working visa or apply for colleges. If they have lived in the United States for such as 3 years or more before reaching 18 years of age and finish college education with Bachelor's degree or join the military, they may be eligible to apply for permanent residence and citizenship later.

8. If businesses such as agricultural or construction companies like to hire special temporary foreign workers from foreign countries directly, they may apply for them through The Department of Homeland Security according to related regulations. If approved, businesses or potential foreign workers need to provide airfare deposits for them to return to their home countries after finishing related temporary work and

9. The processing time and cost to deport illegal immigrants back to their home countries need to be reduced to follow certain practical and efficient procedures. We need to work with foreign country governments properly and teach people to respect and follow our laws.

Illegal immigration (illegal entry, live and work) is a serious problem in many countries. We need to reduce and stop illegal immigrants now and in the future, which increases our national security and reduce or avoid some crimes and potential illegal immigrants to die through the desert and oceans. More foreigners whether visitors, students, legal immigrants, and the special temporary working visa holders come to the United States legally to avoid illegal entry, which supports our national security.

It is reported that about 25,000 students without legal status attend California colleges and cost taxpayers $200 million per year [30]. Many illegal immigrants have gone to California from other states and foreign countries and gotten related welfare programs for many years. The California government has a budget shortage for the past several years, which has become serious problems in California.

Many foreign students come to the United States legally and study for Bachelor, Master or PhD with expensive tuitions, which are higher than in state and out of state tuitions. They contribute to our economic and education systems. Most of these graduates prefer to stay here and work for the U.S. companies. They need to compete with local people and college graduates and follow the U.S. restrictive regulations and economic situations. Only small portion of them can get their jobs with H-1 working visa legally and may apply for permanent residence later according to the U.S. immigration law. Most of foreign students go back to their home countries.

Democratic Party (Labor Party or similar political parties) leaders often consider poor illegal immigrants as their potential voters if they can become citizens. From a political view, the answer is "yes". For a national security, economic balance, and social stability, illegal immigration problem needs to be resolved or limited to reduce future illegal immigrants and terrorists coming to the United States. Illegal immigrants need to respect the U.S. laws. Most illegal immigrants come to the United

States to work for economic reasons. We may use some economic methods to resolve or reduce related problems. For illegal immigrants, who have worked in the United States, we may help them to go back and retire in their countries, in which the portion of their own contributions to social security and Medicare may be used to help them to live in their own countries. They may influence their people. More and more people in their countries may know actual situations in the United States, which will be helpful to reduce future illegal immigrants, and do more to improve their own countries.

Each country has poverty problem. If we consider the poverty issue as a political issue, then more and more populations of the poor would be produced in our country, in which illegal immigration plays a major role. Then poverty problems are never be reduced or resolved. Other countries face the same or similar poverty problems, which need to be resolved or reduced by their leaders and people to be working together with personal and social responsibilities. We have to avoid converting many normal issues into political issues. Otherwise these issues will cause serious social conflicts and problems.

John H. Lee

8. RELIGIOUS AND NON-RELIGIOUS FAITHS

Faith and conflict

There are many religious and non-religious faiths in the world. Some faiths already have their histories more than thousand years. Christian, Muslim, Jew, and Buddhism are the four major religious faiths. There are also many non-religious faiths including political faiths. Different people have different faiths and views. Faiths have helped people to have hope, unite more people and improve civilization and moral standard. Faith conflict is also a major factor, which has caused many wars in the world histories. In the recently years, looks the faith conflicts between Jew or Christian and Muslim are the source to many significant conflicts in the world. It is a challenge to overcome faith conflicts and wars, which might be resolved by finding common ground. The key is for different people to find their common ground, which makes peace and may also affect extremists in any faith(s).

Christians consider Bible to be the words of God. Muslims consider the Quran to be the words of God. Bible and Quran were written by the prophets, who were also people. The two tablets of stone with the Testimony (the law and commands) –

the Ten Commandments (Exodus in Bible) were inscribed by the finger of God. Most people have religious needs. Many people with different religion faiths think their religious God is one true God and the gods of other religious faiths are not true.

Looks religious people with Christian, Muslim or Jew consider there is one true God. People have searched God at different angles through their situations and spirits to form different religious faiths. No one religious faith knows all about God. Even in one faith, there are many different branches. Catholicism and Protestantism are two major Christians [31,32]. Catholicism has Catholic Church, Eastern Orthodox Church, Oriental Orthodox Church, Assyrian Church of the East, Anglican Communion, and other churches self-identified as Catholic. Protestantism has Pre-Lutheran Protestants, Lutheranism, Anglican Churches, Reformed Churches, Presbyterianism, Congregationalist Churches, Anabaptists, Brethren, Methodists, Pietists and Holiness Churches, Baptists, Apostolic Churches, Pentecostalism, Charismatics, Neo-Charismatic Churches, African Initiated Churches, United Churches, Religious Society of Friends, Stone-Campbell Restoration Movement, Sabbath-Keeping Churches, Sabbath-Keeping Churches, and others. Muslim has two major factions of Sunnis and Shias. Sunni has branches of maliki, hanafi, shafi'i, and hanbali. The Shia faith split to different branches. The largest branch are the Twelvers, followed by the Zaidi and Ismaili. These groups follow a different line of Imamate [33].

Different people have different faiths, ideas, views, philosophies, and actions. Besides religious people, there are many people, who have non-religious faiths such as materialism, selfish departmentalism, and communism. There also are people, who have no faiths. We have significant challenges to build a good environment for all people to live together peacefully.

Thousand years ago, people including these prophets, had limited scientific and rational knowledge and experience. They considered almost all things into their faith systems. Many natural phenomena such as rain, lighting, flood, tornado, earthquake, day, and night were considered by God. Science, rationality, and technology have been developed significantly for past two hundred years. People know more and more about human beings, natural phenomena, and their development. Many faith doctrines relate to many fields in faith, religion, nature, culture, political issue, moral standard, law, relationship, and other fields. Some doctrines are overlap in different fields.

When one group of people considers another group of people as their enemies and fights for land, power or faith, one absolute way is to kill each other, which often happened before 1900 specially in ancient time and sometimes happen now. The major reason was your enemies would kill you if you did not kill your enemies, which also often were described in Bible and Quran. After 1900 specially after the cold war, the situations change significantly. Peace becomes a major target for many people and countries with different faiths, ideas, social stages, statuses, positions, and others. More and more countries and their leaders and people have learnt gradually that to avoid violence and wars can be done by peace, respect, communication, working together, and not converting faith conflicts into political problems. Religious faiths are originally to connect death (what happen after death?) and universe (how to create or form universe including earth and human beings).

Christians think Jesus came to this world and begun to connect Christian God with some people again and convert them into Christians as God's children. Muslims think Muhammad connected Muslim God with some people and converted them into Muslims as God's children. One major purpose by God is for people to manage things on the earth and possible universe. People with different background and faiths can be friends by our common ground. Peace may convert enemies into non-enemies, cooperators or even friends. One of our major purposes is to manage the earth and around peacefully and responsibly on rational and faithful levels.

To reach peace is the first factor to concern religious and non-religious faiths for different people to live together peacefully at short and long terms. People with different faiths or without faith shall consider common morale standards. Is it true that people with faiths have high morale and value standards and are more peaceful and responsible? We do see many people with faiths are more peaceful and have high morale standard and as well some not. Besides the first factor Peace, near–death experience and righteousness are other factors to consider faiths.

Faiths relate to spirit issues, which should improve people's spirits and hearts, which should not become political issues. The concept of the human spirit is an idea for theological considerations. Science has no comment on whether or not the spirit exists. Faiths are beliefs and not science. There are significant differences between faiths and science. Science is about repeatable facts, which can be explained scientifically. Faiths are beliefs, which are not repeatable. Faiths can change people's attitudes. Governments and societies shall be managed by common and fair laws to cover all people and not controlled by any faith or special group of people. People need to follow common secular laws and submit authorities at first. On the faith level, people have right to believe any non-violent faiths. Positive concepts in faiths can improve our society with more peace and stability.

When we check our histories, some leaders and people use religious and non-religious faiths to cause many conflicts and wars without peace in many countries and the world. Some leaders, who may have or not have faiths, use faith issues for their own purposes and benefits. Some leaders, who do not believe any religious faiths, abuse their power and do not believe they could be punished in their next life after death.

It seems like faith brings more peace, love, and kindness to communities and the world. Many Christians, Muslims, Jews, and Buddhists as well as people with non-religious faiths or without faith have contributed significant amount of peace and kindness to the communities and the world. But when we check the histories of different countries, many pains, damages, and wars were caused by faith differences and conflicts. Why? Here are several reasons:

1. Many faith leaders like to protect and spread their own faiths, often "brain washing" other people into believing their faiths. They forget to give other people the freedom to choose. Faith is a spiritual and personal issue;

2. Extremists in religious and non-religious faiths have become major reasons of conflicts and wars in the world. Their purpose is not for peace but power by violence or war. These extremists think that only their faiths are right and they try to "force" other people to follow them or to destroy other faiths spiritually and physically;

3. Some leaders use faiths for their own power, benefits, positions or/and controls. This way they and their special groups always have the power to control their people, governments or country. So we need to separate power and benefits from religious and non-religious faiths. People need to inspect their leaders' financial and power situations. It is the best for faith leaders to not have any incomes and benefits when they do their faith work because it makes sure that their sole purpose is for their faiths. Also saved funds could be used for more related projects and helping more people. If they work for their members and receive incomes and benefits from their related faith jobs, then their job descriptions need to be clear. Their power needs to be limited and transparent and their

incomes and benefits need to be not more than average or similar to that of their most members, who donate money. What percentage of leaders in religious and non-religious faiths do their work for their faiths only and not for income, benefit and power? One important purpose is to keep their faiths pure;

4. Some faith leaders use poor people and/or young people to fight against non believers. These leaders often mix faiths and facts together to confuse or mislead people;

5. Some leaders make themselves even as idols or "great" leaders and make people to worship or adore them. They use their faiths as a replacement of common or secular laws to judge other people, which causes serious problems and

6. Some leaders do not treat others of different faiths with equal rights and give themselves special power, rights, and benefits.

Final judgment, determining if religious people will go to heaven or hell, only God has the right. People have no right to judge others based on faiths. Faith is a personal matter. Common or secular laws are used to judge people, who have committed to crimes, by government courts. If extremists use "God's right" to abuse power or to kill others, then they would face God's final judgment after their own deaths. Any religious or non-religious groups should keep their faith pure by limiting their power and benefits. If there is life after death, only God has the right to judge dead people.

When we divide many issues and problems into faith, religion, nature, culture, financial issue, benefit sharing, personality, character, custom, political issue, moral standard, law, or relationship rationally and separately, which help people to convert complex problems into simple issues. Then we can see and analyze issues and problems clearly for proper solutions. But some leaders often mix them together and confuse or mislead people for their own purposes.

Internal and external peace

Both internal peace and external peace are important. Internal peace is within the same or similar faith. External peace is between two or more different faiths.

If one faith of a group of people replaces secular laws with their own faith laws, then the faith of the group of people would cause more conflicts and wars with others. Different groups of people, who have different faiths, ideas, and situations, need to use secular laws/rules as the common law, according to our rational and scientific knowledge and experiences as well as respect for each other. Our purpose is to achieve balances for peace. People have rights to believe their own faiths or no faith at all., It is and should always be a personal matter. Any related benefits from governments, society or organizations should not be involved with faith. All people follow secular laws as the common laws.

Societies were very isolated five hundred years ago. It was not easy for people to have mass migrations or immigrations. A major religious or non-religious faith was usually set up by a king or king's family. Other conflicting faiths or standards were usually not allowed in order to avoid conflicts. There are still similar situations in some countries currently. One leader, one faith, and one political party have been used commonly in many countries controlled by one person/family or one special group of people. There may be short-term stability in such countries, but the people have no personal freedom and the potential development in those controlled situations is limited. The final goal is to reach long-term stability and peace. Technologies have been rapidly developed during the past two hundred years in most areas in the world. Communication, migration, and immigration are becoming much easier now.

People may have three levels. On the first level, people need to deal with each other directly under common secular laws. Secular laws or values are based on science and rationality, which are repeated in different situations. On the second level, or the faith level, people whether they have faith or not need to have peace each other. On the universe or God level, which may be already there by supernatural power or by natural power, is currently beyond human understandings. There are limited natural resources on our earth, which will be used up someday in the future. Also our populations grow every year. We might need or create another place that is similar to our earth where we can live. We will learn more and more about how our earth was created or formed. Then we will know more and more about the natural or supernatural methods, which can help us to find, build or form another "earth".

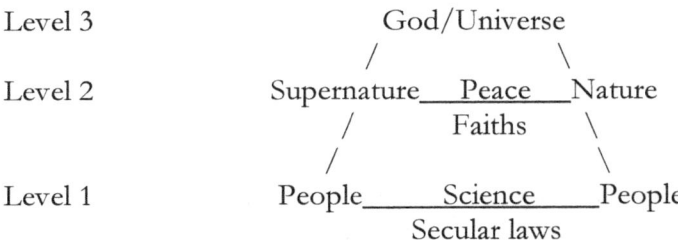

Level 3	God/Universe
Level 2	Supernature___Peace___Nature
	Faiths
Level 1	People___Science___People
	Secular laws

On faith level, there may be these possibilities: (1) there is only one God; (2) there are more gods or (3) God or gods and their doctrines are created by people. It is the freedom of the people to have faiths, whether to be religious, non-religious, or have no faith at all. People with different faiths or no faith may affect their ideas, attitudes, reviews, philosophies, and actions. Our goal is to balance different people with different faiths in order to live together with peace, respect and responsibility. People may have different backgrounds, nationalities, races, cultures, faiths, positions, and situations. Human beings also have "natural" common senses in our minds and hearts, which should be as a common ground for secular laws. Science, rationality and faith can be used to resolve our issues and problems. People have both goodness and sin, but should respect each other in order to have peace together under fair secular laws and freedom with balances.

Now more and more people accept that all humans are from the same source or family, which have been proved scientifically by the Human stone. Christians and Jews believe that the first family was from Adam and Eve. Then more and more people were produced from them. Then people began to spread to different areas, such as the Mideast, Europe, Asia, Africa, and other locations. Cold, mild or warm weather, sunlight, and different environments have affected the human race over a long time, forming white, yellow and black races, a process known as evolution. It is still not fully understood and is difficult to repeat. There are lots of questions that need to be answered about creation and evolution, but to answer is currently beyond humans' ability and will be known more and more. Different people are brothers and sisters originally.

Death and near-death experience

Spiritual life after physical death is the major issue for religions for several thousands of years. People with religious faiths believe that there is another life after death, which allows religious people to face death with a positive hope. People with no religious faith, believe that there is no life after death and often consider death as turning a light bulb from on to off. Different religions have different beliefs regarding life after death, which may affect people's attitudes, values, and behaviors. Death is a mystery and nobody knows what happens because dead people cannot return to this world to tell us. Science has no comment on whether or not the spirit exists. We cannot currently detect spiritual scientific evidence for life after death. Also there is no detail descriptions in holy or religious books. People with different religions live by religious faiths.

Some leaders of faiths, are similar to politicians who promise benefits to voters, even promise idealistic things or benefits for their followers that allow them to fight for their faiths after death or for these followers' families to fight for their faiths after their deaths. But these leaders usually do not go to fight directly by themselves. These leaders often promise things to very simple people, especially young people, who lack life experience and rationality.

Is there a common ground between people of different faiths about death? A key issue about near-death experiences, which belongs between science and faiths, may balance different people as a common ground. Near-death experiences occur during clinical death where a person has no heart beat and is not breathing, which is different from hallucinations. People, who have hallucinations from dreams or drugs, are still breathing and have a beating heart. When people overdose on drugs, they may stop breathing and heart beating. Then they may enter a near-death experience stage. Another significant difference between near-death experiences and hallucinations is about vision. In hallucinations there are many repetitive memories that lack ground in reality and are without vision. In near-death experiences, people's spirits often leave their bodies and they claim to see their own bodies, doctors, nurses, the surrounding environments, and others exactly. There may be the three major factors to affect near-death experiences. Besides the "nature" of the near-death experience itself, there are other two factors, which are environments (including compounds produced by human body) and people themselves. Faith, background, behavior, attitude, and others contribute to a near-death experiences. Some of them are unchangeable and others are changeable. People are responsible for their own near-death experiences, which effects changeable contributions.

Near-death experiences have been studies by many researchers and doctors in the United States, Europe, and Asia. More information is available on the webs. Dr. Raymond Moody studied more than one hundred people, who experienced "clinical death" and had been revived, and published his book "Life after Life" in 1975 [34]. He discussed his investigation of near-death experiences. There are evidences from near-death experiences that the dying people continue to have conscious awareness of their environments after being pronounced clinically dead. The people have experienced spirits outside their physical bodies, seeing themselves and their environments, with light, feeling peace and coming back, which may take up to a period of time at least. The website at www.nderf.org (Near Death Experience Research Foundation) is a good source for near-death experiences. Near-death experience is a practical reality, which may become a common ground for people with religious and non-religious faiths or have no faith at all. Everyone, whether they have religious faiths, non-religious faiths, or no faith, may face near-death experiences. It has been "scientifically" proven by many people including myself, who have had near-death experiences. Some people may argue that near-death experiences are hallucinations. However during hallucinations, related people still have breathing and heart beating. During near-death experiences, related people are in a state of "clinical death", where there is no breathing and heart beating.

According to these experiences and studies, near-death experiences is a phenomenon that happens prior to actual death, in which the person may die or come back to "life". Near-death experiences last much longer than "turning a light bulb from on to off" at least. People do have spirits. A spirit is a special energy. After near-death experiences, there are two possibilities. One possibility is that the spirit may continue to an external life after death, which is favorable outcome for religious people. Another possibility is that the spirit may disappear into air as the special energy transferred into the environment, which is a favorable outcome for non-religious people. Near-death experiences are a true feeling, proved to be part of the pre dying process.

Suicide terrorism and near-death experience

Suicide killings/bombings have happened in past many years, especially becoming a serious problem in the world currently. Suicide killers/bombers often think that they are heroes before their killings. Suicide killings/bombings are a significant challenge to prevent physically. Suicide killers/bombers usually have more power since they posses a knife, gun or bomb before their killings. When a suicide killer/bomber kills other people as well as the self, all the related people face their near-death experiences of their spirits. There is no extra power in a near-death experience, such as a knife, gun or bomb since all spirits face each other fairly. If a suicide killer kills ten people, his or her spirit needs to face other ten spirits during their near-death experiences. These spirits are aware of the killing process. If there is spirit fight between a killer and the victims, then its rate would be one against ten. A peaceful near-death experience is up to self behaviors to a certain degree.

A near death experience may be affected by the environment as well as personal factors, such as faith, behavior, background, age, health, situation, etc. Within these factors, faith and behavior are two important factors. As we know from many near-death experiences, people with peaceful faiths and good behavior when they are in life, usually have peaceful and good near-death experiences.

When Seung-Hui Chu killed thirty-two people in Virginia on April 16, 2007 [35], all individuals had near-death experiences. Near-death experience is a pre-process of dying, which lasts a period of time at least. The thirty-two spirits had the ability to be aware of their bodies and the environments. It is believed

116

that their spirits still had the awareness of the killer's action, according to the records and analysis. Soon Chu killed himself. In Chu's near-death experience, he would see thirty-three dead bodies because of his actions. At this point Chu's spirit would not have the power to carry his gun and would have to face the other thirty-two spirits. In their near-death experiences, Chu's spirit was too weaker when compared with the other thirty-two spirits. It would be very difficult for Chu's spirit to win and to have peace in his near-death experience.

Suicide bombings have often happened in Iraq since 2003. When a suicide bomber kills twenty people before killing self, soon he or she and the twenty people all have near-death experiences. The killer's spirit has to face the other twenty spirits. All twenty-one spirits should have ability to see, recognize, and react during their near-death experiences. If the suicide bomber had a religious faith and thought he could have reward in his life after death, his god also needs to face the twenty spirits, who follow him and complain to him. They are civil victims. Some victims in the twenty people may have his or her same or similar religious faith.

Here are some comments for a potential suicide killer. If you have no religious faith and have "hate" in your mind, then you may have the thought of killing other people and yourself later. But you will face other spirits in your near-death experience. You will not have any extra power, such as gun, in your near-death experience. If you feel that life is unfair and have "hate" in your life, which is from the past, then know that conflicts can be resolved peacefully. Meditation or prayer for a period of time may help you to have more patience, wisdom, and self control, allowing you to deal with these conflicts and have more peace. To take legal action is another option. If you are only focusing on past, not doing anything to improve, then it is almost impossible to have a better future. History should belong to the past. Our focus is the present and the future. The first person to do something to improve the situations would be especially blessed. Becoming a suicide killer because you have had an "unfair" in the past and no peace while also having to face other spirits in your near-death experience. If you have an extreme religious faith, which is a faith issue, you will need to face reality in your near-death experience. If you kill other people and yourself, you will have to face other spirits, who are civil victims of your crime and some of which may have a similar or same religious faith. Then God would not give you a reward in the front of other victim spirits. If you think that other people of a similar or same faith consider you a "hero" because of your suicidal action, then you need to think about your own near death-experience and how you will have to face victims' spirits. There may be one true God for all religious people. Different people were all brothers and sisters originally. In your near death-experience, you will have no extra power, such as a gun or bomb. It is almost impossible for your spirit to have peace with other spirits in your near-death experience. Please respect other people and yourself.

There are many factors that affect near-death experiences, some of them are affected by personal faith, background, behavior, attitude, and others. People will be responsible for their own near-death experiences when they are in life. People whether Christian, Islamic, Jewish, Buddhist or non-religious have a common value of peace. Everybody may have near-death experiences during the dying process. Having peace or not is up to you to a certain degree. If you have no religious faiths, would you please think about how your ideas, attitudes, and behaviors affect your near-death experience. You also need to think about how for your relatives, friends, coworkers will remember you after your death. If you have a religious faith, you need to consider both your near-death experience and your external life after physical death. People, whether with religious faiths or not, need to consider having peace in near-death experiences.

9. COUNTRY DEVELOPMENT AND UNITED NATIONS

Leaders and people in almost all countries have the same goal, having a stable and rich country. How are they to get there? Country development takes effort, understanding, and time for leaders and people to work together.

Four stages for country development

The countries of the past have had many different forms and names. Some of them were pleasing to the ear, containing words like democratic, republic, or peaceful kingdom. In reality there are four major stages of development: a country controlled by one person/family, a country controlled by one group/class, a country controlled/managed by the people (people's country), and a peaceful country.

When power and social resources are controlled by a single person or family in a country, people are forced to obey the ruler and it is easy for power to be abused. The ruler can control the people and kill opponents. There are usually strong dictatorships in a country controlled by one person or family, which is why one king or dictator is usually replaced with another by violence or war.

When power and social resources are controlled by one group or class in a country, this stage of development is an improvement of the country that is ruled by one person or family. However it is still easy for one group of people to abuse their power. These leaders often try to control their people and put their opponents to prison or death, which may lead a short term "peace" without long-term peace. Again when a group or class replaces another, it is usually through violent means.

In a country managed by the people, both the leaders and the people want to build a stable and peaceful country with fair policies and laws, which are very important for the long term stability and peaceful development of that country. During this stage of development, country leaders are generally elected, selected or hired from the people and by the people or their representatives. But the system is still not mature enough for completely peaceful development. Leaders and people still seek their own agendas. Conflict with minor violence is still a problem in these countries. In a peaceful country, the economic, political, and legal systems are very mature. It is truly a country that operates from the people, by the people, and for the people. Leaders and their opponents have peaceful debates for fair and balanced policies in a good democratic environment. They are responsible, with good moral standards, and work together for their country and peaceful development.

The inner workings of a country are far more important than the name of the country. When country's name includes words such as democratic, republic, or peaceful kingdom, their countries should be people's countries or peaceful countries, which means from the people, by the people, and for the people. Country development from a one-person/family controlled country or a one-group/class controlled country to a people's country or a peaceful country with peace without violence and wars will be the best because their country development is at low social costs. There are their transition forms between two developmental stages.

Some country leaders like to control power and become rich much earlier than their people, which may indicate dictatorships. Dictatorships cause more conflicts, serious social problems, violence, and even wars.

Each country has its own history, which needs to be respected by its people and other countries. These histories often define how a country becomes a people's country or a peaceful country. This transition happens when humans look for equal rights, freedom, democracy, responsibility, and common law. People and their leaders need to work together in order to have peaceful country development at low social cost as possible.

A country should not belong to any person, family, party or special group of people. It should belong to all people. Governments should be from the people, by the people, and for the people, having administrations that provide fair and balanced policies for all people regardless of background, income, faith, race, culture, situation, view or philosophy, helping to allow people to live together peacefully and responsibly. Under these fair policies and laws, people should have an equal right for opportunities, develop their personal potential, and become good citizens with good moral standards. Both the people and the government need to be responsible. For economic situation, people should take their own responsibilities, balancing their incomes, expenses, savings, taxes, and donations for both of short and long terms.

Most people and governments would like to build a democratic system that provides equal rights, fair policies, transparency, respect, freedom, and peace at a low social cost. New or potential leaders usually support building a better system than the systems of prior leaders. However, as soon as these new leaders get in the leadership position, they often want to control their newfound power, sometimes even abusing it to benefit themselves. People have two sides, one of goodness and one of sin. It is best to build a social system where people can express their goodness and have self control when it comes to expressing their sin, which is good for themselves, their families, and their countries. Dictatorships often replace prior dictatorships by sinful means. The abuse of power, corruption, and unfair policies are prevalent in dictated countries, which produces even more conflict and causes violence and war, which come at a high social cost. These leaders and their countries have more social problems including corruption, low efficiency, complain, violence, and potential war. Being a democratic country not only means that leaders are elected, selected or hired from the people and by the people peacefully, but also that these leaders respect the people and their country and laws, resulting in peaceful development without serious social problems like corruption and power abuse. Leaders need to be inspected and be transparent in their actions. Then their country and society can be managed with stable and peaceful development at a good social efficiency and low social cost.

Many people and countries are afraid of dictators and want to prevent dictatorships. Two significant reasons are that dictators can start wars and movements without approval from the people or their congress and kill people without a reasonable court trial. We need to limit the power of leaders and dictators, letting them and their people work together to convert their countries into stable people's and peaceful countries.

Balanced governance

Countries, whether in a one-person/family controlled country, one-group controlled country, or people's country, would all need balanced governance. Balanced governance means that the government has efficient operations, at as low of a social cost as possible, while still meeting the interests and needs of the people and the nation. Food and life quality for all people should be the first and basic target of governments. Proper distribution of taxes is important for country development, which should be discussed and rebated to balance different groups of people and their benefits. Governments need to have fair and transparent policies to prevent and punish corruption. One efficient example would be to inspect leaders' assets and incomes. To avoid the wasting or stealing of social resources, governments need to have administrations that support the people and the government mutually instead of serving political purposes. Foreign policy is to balancing peace and national defense. Reasonable cost is used to develop military technologies. Modern military methods have been improved significantly, which are totally different from the situations fifty years ago. We need to have more wisdom in order to convert enemies into non enemies and cooperators to avoid or reduce conflicts and wars. To create internal and external enemies politically causes more damage to the people, countries and the world, while also costing more social resources. During the Cold War, many countries from both the east and west were considered enemies because of the lack of good communication. Some of these enemies were created for political purposes by leaders. Fairly short and long-term policies can create balanced, stable, and peaceful country development.

Each country has its own situation, meaning that different fair and practical policies need to be studied and developed at low social cost for each country. Leaders and people need to think what their country could and should be after 50 or 100 years. Making their country into a balanced, stable, and peaceful country is a major goal. No matter what stage a country is at, balanced governance is needed. Balanced governance means:

(1) to balance the peoples' interests and national interests;

(2) to be transparent and efficiently inspecting for prevention of corruption;

(3) to be concerned to improve people's life quality;

(4) to make fair economic and political policies as possible and improve their systems gradually;

(5) to balance government size, people's needs, and government spending;

(6) to make fair short and long-term policies to balance different people's interests and benefits as possible;

(7) to have effective security and military needs at a reasonable cost and to teach people to respect laws;

(8) to balance administration function with as little political purpose as possible;

(9) to make fair foreign policies with flexibility to balance national and foreign interests and peace and

(10) to achieve a balanced, stable, and peaceful development.

Balanced country systems with laws are able to receive respect and peace, which can avoid or reduce many problems and promote peaceful development. Lack of transparency and inspection system lead to government corruption, inefficient operations, and high social costs, which are major problems in country development. Democratic elections from the people and by the people or their representatives are good, which is not enough. Social costs and many negative effects are also needed to be considered and reduced. In many developing countries without enough social resources, leaders may be selected or hired by the peoples' representatives at low social costs. It is of utmost importance that leaders balance their services to people under fair policies in their countries. In many countries of Eastern Europe, Africa, or Asia, democratic elections have been used for many years, which mean government leaders are elected by the people politically. It is more important for government leaders to balance and serve their people. Leaders, even those who are elected by people, often abuse their power and have corruption if there is no complete system of transparency and inspection. People's interests are often not respected and their life quality is not improved by their leaders. These situations need to be improved. Of course the transition from dictatorship to democracy involves building a democratic system, which takes time and effort.

Government size is a critical issue, which is one of major fight points for liberals and conservatives. Liberals like to have large governments to reach and help more low-income and poor people. Major government operation costs are from taxes of companies and rich and mid-income people. Large governments also mean more power for government leaders. Conservatives like to have limited governments and people need to take more personal responsibilities, which means to reduce taxes. Then rich and mid-income people and companies will have more freedom to use their money for different purposes including job creations. Personal responsibilities can create more taxes and business opportunities. To help disable and poor people with real needs is needed. To reduce poverty by personal responsibilities is needed, too. We need to balance these factors and build efficient government operations at low cost as possible. We also need to take care disabled and poor people with real needs after their personal responsibilities. Government budgets need to be balanced.

Indian has become an independent country since 1947. Then western-style political system has been used in Indian. After more than sixty years, Indian is still considered as a poor developing country. One of major reasons is that some government officers have had corruption problems and not used more social resources for their people. Some leaders have used poor people for their voting purpose. Before votes, they liked to give poor people many promises, in which most promises were not really recognized later. They have used public office positions for their own benefits. These officers are

John H. Lee

"dirty" politicians. Then the efficiency of government operations is low. There are many non-profit organizations and people such as Mother Teresa spent long time to work for the poor people. Their results are not significant because they have limited social resources. Common people need to take more personal responsibilities and to push government officers for their real reform to improve government operations. When the ten terrorists attacked Bombay on November 26, 2008, it was too later for Indian armed forces to react and deal with the terrorists. After four days, then nine terrorists were killed and one terrorist was captured. The terrorism caused about 200 people died, 300 people injured, fire and construction damages. The governance in Indian was weak.

The People's Republic of China has significant changes and improvement in the past thirty years. Poverty was a serious problem in the country before 1980, which has been improved significantly because of the major reasons such as relatively peaceful environment, personal potential development, capitalism development besides socialism, low-cost labors, government policy and leadership improvement. The country also has several significant challenges such as economic stability, political reform, government corruption, unstable and unfair policies, human right, investment and intelligent immigration, moral standard reduction, true/false information confusion, difference between city and countryside, conflicts between rich and poor people, population, and unbalanced rate of males to females. During past thirty years, The People's Republic of China had become major factories for many other countries and exported their goods. Since 2009, the country has difficulties because of the international financial crisis and lack of enough international market, which has affected China. Looks its internal market development will become a new target in the country. There are more conflicts between governments and people relate to land, properties, tax distributions, living cost increase, medical services, and corruptions. One of their challenges is how to balance personal/company and government interests with proper distributions of social resources and build transparent inspection and harmonious and balanced social environment.

Another significant challenge is for The People's Republic of China and Taiwan (Republic of China) how to have peace together. The People's Republic of China wants to unite (some leaders in The People's Republic of China want to liberate Taiwan with force and war). Taiwan (Republic of China) does not want to be united or wants to be independent if possible. This serious issue really needs leaders and people at the two sides to develop their potential wisdom to resolve the issue peacefully. The current Taiwan (Republic of China) government presents "No Independent, No United, and No War" policy to stabilize the relationship. Almost all people at the both sides want to have peace. Looks there may be three steps for both sides to reach peace and united progress gradually, which take exchange, negotiation, time, wisdom, balance, and work together: (1) to make peaceful development together; (2) to convert The People's Republic of China and Taiwan (Republic of China) into one country with the two governments (or two areas) of China: People's Republic (The Mainland) and China: Republic (Taiwan) and then into (3) to become one country with one government: China (Zhonghua in Chinese) with significant adjustments and political reform gradually and peacefully. The key factor is for balanced and peaceful development.

In country development, some people and leaders often simply divide capitalism and socialism into totally separated systems, which may be a serious mistake and have extremely trend with strong political concepts. Looks there might be still a potential trend for different countries to form capitalism allies and socialism allies in the world, which needs to be avoided in the future. Capitalism has advantages and disadvantages. Under capitalism, freedom market adjusts economic situations. Good products at reasonable prices are preferred by people to lead market. People innovate new products and services for more opportunities and benefits. Looks this is the best model to develop people's potential and hard work for economic development. But capitalism puts money (profit) to the first factor. Poor people may lack of training, opportunity, right, and improvement. It is easy for business owners or companies to make money without considering reasonable employees' benefits and social responsibility special in early stage of economic development. Worker unions often consider more workers' benefits and their own fees and not balance employers' factors, which usually cause high production costs. Employers often move their production to low-cost countries or areas. High unemployment may cause strong social conflicts. Socialism also has advantages and disadvantages. Under socialism, governments pay more attention to social service, food needs, and life quality for poor people, and military development. But government officers have more power and like to keep their power and benefits, which usually cause them to control product production, price, management, social resource, living conditions, and education and to not respect laws and people. Then governments provide less and less rights to people. People have less or no space to develop personal potentials and creativities. Both living standard and competition become lower and lower. Government operations lack of transparent inspection, which usually cause government corruption. People and their countries usually become poor on long term. When people know more truths, they will have different opinions from their leaders and like to have more equal rights. Poor people are often called by opponent leaders to have class warfare, which will damage their country, people, and social environments significantly. During country development, many issues such as capitalism and socialism can be balanced to have both advantages, which are possible to reach better achievements.

In modern countries, capitalism and socialism are balanced and combined for their advantages. Individuals can develop their potentials and responsibilities. Countries make fair policies to protect human rights, freedom, and social services such as minimum wage, unemployment benefits, and basic living standard. Capitalism is the foundation for people to develop their personal potentials, for companies to innovate new products and services and for a society to have abundant resources. Socialism provides social services to help disabled and poor people with real needs, give children good education, make necessary regulations, utilize social resources and provide strong military and security to protect their country and stabilize peace in the world. For example the "Self-Support" social security system, which is described in Chapter 2, is a good example to combine capitalism and socialism together. Let most people to be responsible for their own social security earnings and payments. Governments help the poor with real needs with the extra social security taxes over a maximum payment from high incomers.

Countries shall consider both short and long-term visions for peaceful development. To develop countries into stable, peaceful, and rich countries at low social costs are needed to be considered by leaders and people. We need to have balanced governance with real contents at low social costs as possible.

Peaceful development and United Nations

We can learn many lessons from our histories in different countries in such as Europe and Asian. From one dynasty to another dynasty or one king to another king with dictatorships in many countries were done by violence or wars, which have shown by our histories over thousand years. These wars have caused significant social costs such as one dynasty change killed million people and damaged environments, social systems, orders, people's normal life, security, laws, and governments seriously, even same dictator' family members fought or killed each other for getting more power. Only both leaders and people commit to peaceful or non-violence improvement to the next stages to become people's or peaceful countries and keep stable and peace under laws, respect, transparency, freedom, and democratic system are at the lowest social costs, which are good for countries, people, leaders, and the world. Many countries in Europe and Asia already have good examples to work together and convert their countries from one person/family controlled countries into people's countries with low social costs. One hundred sixty years ago, there were many slaves in the United States. Then the U.S. leaders and people overcame related difficulties and worked together to become a people's country. There are also many countries, their people have already paid significant price at very high social costs with violence and wars, are still in one person/family or one group/party controlled country stage. Their leaders and people do really need to make plans to overcome difficulties and make progress for peaceful country development.

Almost all dictators in our histories have been punished or criticized by people before or after their deaths. Histories give fair evaluations and descriptions for leaders by truths before, now, and future. Before leaders become dictators, they also usually support to build fair social systems against their prior leaders or dictators, in which some of these leaders often are national heroes. After leaders are in their top positions for short terms, they may do something good for their people such as building constructions, making fair policies, let people to develop their potential, and giving reasonable rights back to people. Then later they often like to have more power and dictatorship for more benefits for themselves and control people. Power abuse, corruption, and unfair policies usually happen in dictated countries.

Moammar Gadhafi was a hero in his country Libya. Gadhafi led a group of military officers on September 1, 1969 against King Idris of Libya while the king was in Turkey for medical treatment. Then Gaddafi was Libya's dictator for 42 years until he was ousted in an uprising-turned-civil war. He and his family owned huge assets, properties, and cash through his power. The international war crimes court issued an arrest as against Moammar Gadhafi in June, 2011. The 69-year-old Moammar Gadhafi was killed in his hometown on October 20, 2011 [36].

In January, 2011, Haitian authorities questioned former dictator Jean-Claude Duvalier and might prosecute him for stealing from the treasury during his rule. He fled Haiti in 1986 to escape a popular uprising [37].

Zine El Abidine Ben Ali was appointed Tunisian Prime Minister in October 1987. He assumed the Presidency on November 7, 1987 in a bloodless coup against President Habib Bourguiba, who was declared incompetent. Then Ben Ali ruled Tunisia from 1987 to 2011. On January 14, 2011, following a month of violent protests against his rule, Ben Ali was forced to flee to Saudi Arabia along with his family. The Tunisian government charged him for money laundering and drug trafficking and asked an international arrest warrant. He and his wife were sentenced in absentia to 35 years in prison on June 20, 2011 [38]. If Ben Ali were to commit and announce in 2010 or early 2011 that he would become the last dictator and work with his people (including opponents) to have Tunisia into stable and peaceful development with good governance as possible, his country might begin peaceful development after his announce. He would become one of great leaders in his country and the world.

Egypt's President Hosni Mubarak [39] gave the world a good example to work with his people, step down and quit his power after many protesters pushed him to give away his power back to people after his 30 years in power. Although it was some later, he still gave a possible chance for future peaceful and smooth to transfer power in Egypt. Poverty was a key issue for Egyptians to angry to their leader. Egyptians need peaceful development for their country. Yemen's President Ali Abdullah Saleh [40] resigned to step down after 33 years in power in 2011 is another good example to avoid more violence or war if Yemen's people and leaders can work together peacefully. Of course people and leaders need to work together to have their balanced and good governance, and peaceful development for their country, which take time, understanding, effort, forgiveness, and tolerance. If leaders transfer their power positively and regularly, peaceful social transitions without violence or war are the best with minimum social costs and have safe and stable social orders. When both government leaders and people work together from up to down and from down to up peacefully, then their performance will be the best for peaceful development. One key factor is to build mature democratic systems to avoid dictatorships in the future.

Another serious issue for many countries is North Korea, which has nuclear weapon. The North Korean government announced on December 19, 2011 that the "Dear Leader", "our Father" and "the General" Kim Jong-il died at 69 years old on December 17, 2011 because of his "physical and mental over-work" on a train on his way to give field guidance to factories, farms, and the military [41]. His youngest son, Kim Jong-un at about later twenties is as the "Great Successor" and "the outstanding leader of the party, army, and people". Many countries special South Korea, the United States, China, Russia, and Japan have great attention to the stability of the country. One challenge is how for other countries to deal with North Korea effectively for the peaceful development for this country and the world. At first we need to study the recent history (about hundred years) of North Korea.

By the late 19th century, Korea was the colonial under Japan until the end of World War II in August 1945. Korea was affected and bullied by foreign countries from past hundred years to 1948. In 1945, the Soviet Union declared war on Japan. The Red Army churned into Pyongyang with almost no resistance. The United States occupied the south. The United Nations divided Korea at the 38th parallel into South Korea and North Korea in 1945. In September 1945, Kim Il-sung [42] was installed by the Soviets as head of the Provisional People's Committee. Original plan was for all-Korean elections, which was sponsored by the United Nations. The South declared statehood as the Republic of Korea in May, 1948 [43]. The Democratic People's Republic of Korea was proclaimed in September, 1948 by the North. Kim Il-sung served as the premier. On October 12, 1948, the Soviet Union declared that Kim's regime was the only lawful government on the peninsula. New People's Party, The Communist Party, and the Workers Party of Korea were combined into Workers Party of North Korea. Kim Il-sung served as the party chairman.

Kim Il-sung took the steps to let his people to build "faithful" minds.

1.   Let North Koreans to know he was "genius" and "powerful" as their Great Leader. Only he could help North Koreans against strong foreign enemies and give them better life from poor conditions. North Koreans have had the significant concern about foreign enemies, who may occupy their land and bully them according to their history;

2.   Told or brain washed his people that the United States was their No. #1 enemy, who would attack North Korea anytime. Only "Great Leader" and "General" Kim Il-sung could protect them, which converted people to trust him. Without him, people did not know how to deal with their enemies (It was main reason why people cried so much when Kim Il-sung passed away);

3.   Closed his country from the outside world. Individual migrations and immigrations were controlled;

4.   Built a special group of people from top to bottom and from bottom to top, who share benefits from the central government. Control from top to bottom and obey from

bottom to top well. All important decisions were done by "Great Leader".

5.　　Told North Koreans only Kim Il-sung liked them to know. Opponents were not allowed with serious punishments;

6.　　Controlled power, media, people, and almost everything. TV and newspapers were controlled by the government. Newspapers and TV broadcasted there were many poor people (homeless individuals) with terrible living conditions to represent most people in such as the United States and South Korea, which gave North Koreans to feel their life were already relatively good enough and

7.　　Made "military first" policy and spent more social resources for soldiers and weapon development. There were less social resources used for economic purposes to improve people's life quality. Let North Koreans to prepare to have a war anytime, in which solider populations were very high. Let North Koreans to have duty to liberate South Koreans and occupy South Korea someday in the future.

Kim Il-sung ruled North Korea from 1948 to his death in 1994. From 1974 to his death, he trained and promoted his son Kim Jong-il, who also claimed "genius" and "powerful" as the supreme leader of North Korea. Kim Jong-il succeeded his father Kim Il-sung following the elder Kim's death in 1994. Kim Jong-il was the General Secretary of the Workers Party of North Korea, Chairman of the National Defense Commission of North Korea, and the supreme commander of the Korean People's Army. In 2010, Forbes Magazine's List of The World's Most Powerful People in 2010, Kim Jong-il was ranked the 31st in the list.

Most dictators also pay attention and study other countries and the world. They like to develop their countries, increase production, and provide better living conditions to their people, in which they need to control the power and do not like to lose their power at first. They are afraid of their people to know more truths and override their dictatorships, which have often happened in many countries. So they do not allow their people to know more truths in their country, from other countries, and around the world through internet, TV, newspapers, and radio with restrict controls. Nuclear weapon development is their preference. Then they have negotiation power with other countries special their "enemies". They can also show to their people to be protected and defended. They usually would not use those weapons to attack other countries at first because they know their weapon quality and quantity are much less than their "enemies".

Some Americans like to remove the dictators in some countries by some strong actions, which seems to liberate those people. It will be a significant wrong idea. At first they are independent countries. Also related costs are very high. The key is that most people in those countries such as North Korea do not agree and consider the United States as their No.1 enemy currently in their minds and will fight against the United States for their "Great Leader" and country, which we cannot understand if without deep considerations. Most North Koreans are afraid of the United States and South Korea to attack them. Here is one story in North Korea, which may explain something. It was reported that a small group of American doctors went North Korea to treat and cure patients in their voluntary trips. After these patients special with serious diseases such as low-vision blind were cured, they thanked to their "Great Leader" with tears at first. Seemed the "Great Leader" sent the American doctors to take care these patients.

On February 29, 2012, North Korea agreed to suspend its uranium-enrichment program and long-range missile tests. Under the agreement with the above condition, the U.S. would ship 20,000 tons of food to North Korea each month for a year. Soon North Korea announced on March 16, 2012 to launch a satellite called Kwangmyongsong-3 (Shining Star) into orbit for the 100th anniversary of the birth of the regime's founder, Kim Il Sung. North Korea announced the satellite was their plan, which was agreed by former "Great Leader" and "General" Kim Jong-il and "We believe the satellite launching will be absolutely successful under the personal guidance from Kim Jong-un". North Korea considered to launch the satellite for peaceful purpose and not relate to long-range missile tests in its announcement and complained the United States have not followed the prior agreement about the food. The satellite launch, which might cost more than $150 million, was failed during the launching after few minutes, which made North Korea even further isolated from other countries [44-46]. The United States stopped to ship the food because of the satellite launching.

How to deal with North Korea or similar countries for peaceful development is a significant challenge. Here are some comments.

1.   To add the details including for North Korea to agree to suspend such as satellite and nuclear power plant into the uranium-enrichment program and long-range missile tests in the prior agreement, which are clear to be understood publically. A waiting period of time such as half or one year is required for North Korean to not do any above uranium-enrichment program, long-range missile, and satellite, then the United States will continue the prior food supplies. If the food supplies are for feeding children, mothers, pregnant women, and the elderly (not to North Korea's elites or military), the United States may send responsible persons (more volunteers from South Korea and China if needed) to distribute the food supplies to related North Koreans, which may also be considered to improve people-to-people connections. It is reported about 150 American musicians of Sons of Jubal chorus and orchestra visited North Korea to perform at the Spring Friendship Art Festival in April, 2012. Global Resource

Services, an Atlanta-based humanitarian group, coordinated the cultural exchange. "The theme of the festival is friendship, and with the conflict between our countries we always think any way we can try to build good will people-to-people that's private, not government, is a good thing to do," said Global Resource Services President Robert Springs. The Spring Friendship Art Festival in North Korea generally attracts between 600 and 800 performers a year from up to 60 different countries [47].

2.   Other countries like China, Russia, Japan, and South Korea may also use similar conditions when they supply food supplies to North Korea.

3.   To discuss a conditional non-attack peaceful agreement such as if North Korea does not develop nuclear weapon and not attack South Korea and the United States at first, then South Korea and the United States will not attack North Korea. Let more and more North Koreans to know the truths, have open minds, and not consider the United States as their No. #1 enemy, who would not attack North Korea with the above condition. It may help North Koreans and their government and leaders to change their main focus from military development to their economic development for basic needs of food and life quality.

4.   Some North Korea government officers may visit other countries such as South Korea, the United States, China, Russia or Japan to learn skills for economic development. They also need to tell North Koreans truths fairly.

5.   Suggest North Korea government to plan stable and peaceful country development including economic and political reforms. North Korea needs to resolve its own economic and political problems peacefully at low social costs as possible;

6.   Suggest North Korea government to give its people

more human right and freedom for personal potential development, which also helps their country. Personal potential development is one of major foundation factors for country development and

7. The United States may consider and promise North Korea and South Korea that after North Korea becomes a people's country and unites with South Korea peacefully, the United States will withdraw its military from South Korea. It also will help Chinese and Russians to think there is no direct military threat from the United States through South Korea and to push their leaders and governments to do more for stable and peaceful development and converting their countries into good people's countries peacefully. China and Russia also play important roles for peace in the world.

Dictators do not like to lose their power and are afraid people to criticize them. Also dictators are quietly busy to make many decisions because of lack of detail and transparent inspections. Although governments have made different laws, these dictators do not respect their laws. They have to lie to their people. Looks they might have two options. One is to continue to do their dictatorship and control their people until they are overridden by people and punished significantly, which is done usually by violence or war. Then another dictatorship is often produced. Another option is for them to make peaceful plans to transfer their partial or all power to their people. But they are afraid their people to know truths and will be overridden and punished into prisons by court trials. Here is an important issue is how to forgive these dictators (or some leaders) without or with less punishment during transitions from one-person/family or one-group/class controlled countries into people's countries. Forgiveness and limiting their power and benefits are helpful during and after the transitions. The peaceful and smoothly power transfer costs the lowest social resources for forming mature systems peacefully and gradually. Then new leaders will follow their systems and improve their systems with more and more mature. Mature systems can prevent leaders to become new dictators.

Current relationships between one-person/family or one-group controlled countries and people's countries have been improved in the past thirty years, which still need to be improved further in the world. Leaders in one-person/family or one-group controlled countries usually make restrict policies to control their people and punish their opponents. Leaders in people's or peaceful countries often complain those leaders in one-person/family or one-group controlled countries to control their people, ask to have more political reform, and support those countries economically after political reform. Effective communications between one-person/family or one-group controlled countries and people's or peaceful countries are very important. Each country has its own situations. When people and leaders know more and more truths, they would make plans and take steps gradually for peaceful development. Country development takes time, understandings, efforts, and patience. Different countries may have different challenges. Their development to people's and peaceful stages may take short or long time such as hundred years. Leaders and people in both one-person/family or one-group controlled countries and people's or peaceful countries need more exchange, dialogue, wisdom, patience, and commitment. Countries shall consider to have balanced governance at first and then to good governance. Countries also shall consider short and long-term visions to have fair systems for peaceful development.

United Nations may provide some professional teams to train leaders in different countries for better leadership skills to balance different factors and people, to avoid power abuse and government corruption, to build balanced or good governance, and to have fair policies for short and long-term peaceful development. To avoid wars between countries, United Nations may mediate/conciliate or reconcile their conflicts.

Political elections usually cost more social resources. Developed countries may have more social resources to spend. To reduce social costs and use social resources wisely in developing countries, leaders may be selected or hired according to such as their background, ability, experience, record, character, and moral standard by people's representatives, who make job descriptions, position length, power limitation, and benefits for their leaders. Another significant issue is for different groups of people to respect each other peacefully. If elections cause fight or violence situations during different groups of people in some countries, then the process to hire leaders by people's representatives may have less fight or violence situations. Whether by election or hiring process, governments (such as legal and revenue departments) and people shall have rights to inspect their leaders' assets, incomes, records, and related situations to prevent government corruptions.

Many countries require people with incomes to file tax returns every year. Also many countries require people with above certain income to file tax return every year. Government leaders/workers, business owners, and executives are required to file tax return for the purpose to prevent their corruptions.

Corruption is a very serious problem in many countries, which costs significant social resources. For example Mayor Johnson gave twenty city projects to different companies and had bribes from these companies. He transferred the bribes to his relatives and friends to avoid direct records. If the investigations took two years, the court finally judged him with seven years in jail. Also his relatives and friends had related punishments. These social costs for Mr. Johnson's case were significant to the government and people in his city. It is very important to prevent corruptions for reducing social costs.

When we check the relationship between these companies and Mayor Johnson, the companies could not get these projects if not offering Johnson bribes. Mayor Johnson had power to give the project(s) to these companies without real normal and fair procedures. He asked related companies to give him bribes through his relatives and friends. The bribe source was from related companies to Mayor Johnson, which was partial cost from their operation costs. Then his city government paid more prices. Besides building a transparent inspection system, another policy is to give related companies another chance. Within a period of time such as two years after receiving government project(s) or offer(s), related companies can release related bribe documents to a courthouse. Then these companies can have no or less punishment and continue their project(s) as usual business. Related government officers need to return all bribes to the government and pay fines. Jail time to related government officers may be necessary according actual cases. If related companies do not release facts within a period of time, then these companies will have full punishment. The purpose is to punish government officers to avoid government corruptions as possible. Bribers and bribees have different function and responsibility. Of course the best is all people respect laws.

In poor countries, people often complain they have no money to buy their foods and goods for their basic life. Business and companies complain to have no money to invest for producing goods for their customers. Governments also often complain they have no money to pay people and to loan businesses and companies. When governments print more money, inflation is significantly negative issue. But when governments print more money and enter it into a circle to companies from loans as investments to production, employment, product/service sale, profit, share, and reinvestment. Then employees can improve their life quality and have more purchase power to support society through their work. Businesses and companies can produce products/services and create value for societies. Companies use partial profit to return to governments or banks gradually.

Governments shall be responsible to control and avoid inflation. During this period of time, company owners shall have their equalities or be limited for their incomes and all records shall be inspected until those loans are returned.

Population is an important factor. When populations grow too fast, more social resources are needed to match. When birth rate reduces significantly, there may be lack of human resource to support families, old people, and social resources after 20-50 years. Proper income and tax distributions to different people are very important to balance people and internal purchasing power for stable and peaceful development. Also balanced policies are needed to protect environments without serious damages for long term.

Many countries have paid too much social costs for their country development. People need to develop their countries into stable, peaceful, and rich countries with low social costs as possible. Wish more and more leaders and people learn from our histories to not abuse power and to have peaceful development for their countries at low social costs.

REFERENCES

[1] http://liheap.ncat.org/profiles/povertytables/FY2010/popstate.htm

[2] http://sec.gov/news/press/2011/2011-267.htm

[3]http://www.usnews.com/news/national/articles/2009/06/29/madoff-sentenced-to-150-years-in-prison

[4] http://www.nytimes.com/2010/12/12/business/12madoff.html?pagewanted=all&_r=0

[5] http://hotair.com/archives/2009/09/22/exclusive-cbo-predicts-social-security-cash-deficits-in-2010-11/

[6] http://cnsnews.com/news/article/cbo-social-security-run-45-billion-deficit-2011

[7] http://independentreport.blogspot.com/2011/02/congress-robbed-social-security-and.html

[8] http://fairmark.com/retirement/socsec/pia.htm

[9] http://www.dailymail.co.uk/news/article-1322441/France-riots-Demonstrations-pension-reforms-continue-ninth-day.html

[10] http://census.gov/compendia/statab/2011/tables/11s0102.pdf

[11] http://learner.org/courses/envsci/visual/visual.php?shortname=life_expectancy_at_birth

[12] http://socialsecurity.gov/planners/lifeexpectancy.htm

[13] http://census.gov/compendia/statab/cats/income_
expenditures_poverty_wealth/family_income.html

[14] http://census.gov: U.S. Census Bureau, Income, Poverty and
Health Insurance Coverage in the United States: 2008, Current
Population Reports, P60-236(RV), and Detailed Tables -- Table
FINC-07, September 2009.

[15] http://www.cbsnews.com/8301-250_162-57344644/senate-
oks-budget-bill-tax-cut-extension/

[16] http:// news.yahoo.com/philippines-struggles-aids-
203739326.html

[17] http://cdc.gov/hiv/resources/factsheets/us.htm

[18]http://who.int/mediacentre/factsheets/fs360/en/index.html

[19] http://ssa.gov/pubs/10043.html#a0=2

[20] http://divorce.com/rising-rate-divorce/

[21] http://www.taxlawtips.com/audits/

[22] 1040 Instructions 2011 by Internal Revenue Service

[23] 1040 Instructions 2021 by Internal Revenue Service

[24] http://news.yahoo.com/blogs/sideshow/michigan-woman-
still-collecting-food-stamps-winning-1-201751693.html

[25] http://www.king5.com/news/local/Feds--Seattle-welfare-
recipient-lived-in-million-dollar-home-134943613.html

[26] http://zh.wikipedia.org/wiki/%E5%9B%BD%E5%85%B1
%E5%86%85%E6%88%98#cite_note-1

[27] http://zhidao.baidu.com/question/408782886

[28] http://en.wikipedia.org/wiki/Chinese_Civil_War

[29] http://www.cbp.org/pdfs/2011/111117_How_Are_Federal_Dollars_Spent_pb.pdf

[30] http://articles.latimes.com/2010/nov/15/local/la-me-illegal-students-20101116

[31] http://en.wikipedia.org/wiki/Christianity

[32] https://en.wikipedia.org/wiki/Catholicism

[33]https://en.wikipedia.org/wiki/Islamic_schools_and_branches

[34] http://en.wikipedia.org/wiki/Raymond_Moody

[35] http://en.wikipedia.org/wiki/Seung-Hui_Cho

[36] https://en.wikipedia.org/wiki/Moammar_Gadhafi

[37]http://topics.nytimes.com/top/reference/timestopics/people/d/jeanclaude_duvalier/index.html

[38] http://en.wikipedia.org/wiki/Zine_El_Abidine_Ben_Ali

[39] http://en.wikipedia.org/wiki/Hosni_Mubarak

[40] http://en.wikipedia.org/wiki/Ali_Abdullah_Saleh

[41] http://en.wikipedia.org/wiki/Kim_Jong-il

[42] http://en.wikipedia.org/wiki/Kim_Il-sung

[43] http://en.wikipedia.org/wiki/Korea#Proto.E2.80.93Three_Kingdoms

[44] http://www.cnn.com/2012/03/16/world/asia/north-korea-satellite-launch/

[45] http://news.sohu.com/s2012/chaoxianweixing/

[46] http://news.sohu.com/20120412/n340316464.shtml

[47] http://news.yahoo.com/us-based-musical-group-performing-north-korea-spring-231235235.html

ABOUT THE AUTHOR AND BOOK

John Lee was laid off because of the bankruptcy of his former employer. After his job search failed, he started a service company with no investment. He has been a small business owner for more than 12 years. He was a teacher before coming to the United States at the age of 28 as a foreign student with different background and language.

He has studied related topics and issues for several years and prepared this book with his views, data, and formulas. His purpose is to provide possible solutions and options for the issues and problems of recession, social security, Medicare, education, personal balance, government policy, tax simplification, faith, social conflict, and country development.